GLOBETROTTER™

Travel Guide

BARBADOS

Melissa Shales

NEW
HOLLAND

NEW
HOLLAND

★★★ Highly recommended
★★ Recommended
★ See if you can

Fourth edition published in 2015
by MapStudio™
10 9 8 7 6 5 4 3 2 1
www.globetrottertravelguides.com

Distributed in Africa by
MapStudio™
Unit 3, Block B, M5 Park, Eastman Road,
Maitland 7405, Cape Town, South Africa
PO Box 193, Maitland 7404

Distributed in the UK/Europe/Asia by
John Beaufoy Publishing Ltd

Distributed in the USA by
National Book Network

ISBN 978 1 77026 661 2

This guidebook has been written by independent authors and
updaters. The information therein represents their impartial
opinion, and neither they nor the publishers accept payment
in return for including in the book or writing more favourable
reviews of any of the establishments. Whilst every effort has
been made to ensure that this guidebook is as accurate and
up to date as possible, please be aware that the facts quoted
are subject to change, particularly the price of food, transport
and accommodation. The Publisher accepts no responsibility
or liability for any loss, injury or inconvenience incurred by
readers or travellers using this guide.

Commissioning Editor: Elaine Fick
DTP Cartographic Manager: Genené Hart
Editors: Elaine Fick, Thea Grobbelaar, Carla Zietsman,
Sean Fraser
Picture Researcher: Shavonne Govender
Design and DTP: Nicole Bannister, Tracey Fraser
Cartographers: Elaine Fick, Inga Ndibongo, Luyolo
Ndlotyeni, Genené Hart

Reproduction by Hirt & Carter (Pty) Ltd, Cape Town
Printed and bound by Craft Print International Ltd, Singapore

Acknowlegdements:
Melissa Shales would like to thank Victoria Gooch, Benedict
Hudson and Tim Richards for their help with researching and
compiling the book, the Barbados Tourist Office in London
and Bridgetown, Xl.com, Elegant Hotels, Almond Resorts,
The Crane, and Treasure Beach Hotel for their generous
help with transport and accommodation, and in particular,
Shernelle Blackman for making many complicated
arrangements superbly, and Emerson, driver extraordinaire
for his skill and company on the journey.

Photographic credits:
www.adamspicturelibrary.com: pages 4, 25, 109;
Barbados Tourism Authority: pages 24, 27, 88; International
Photobank/Jeanetta Baker: page 36; International
Photobank/Peter Baker: title page, pages 30, 35, 39, 60,
103, 112; Buddy Mays: pages 47, 95; Photo Access: pages
32, 85, 86, 100; Melissa Shales: pages 6, 7, 8, 9, 10, 11,
13, 14, 15, 16, 17, 18, 20, 21, 22, 23, 28, 37, 38, 40, 41, 42,
44, 46, 49, 50, 51, 52, 57, 58, 59, 63, 64, 65, 68, 70, 72, 74,
76, 77, 78, 80, 82, 84, 87, 89, 92, 96, 97, 98, 102, 106, 107;
Shutterstock: page 101; Travel Pictures Ltd: cover, pages 26,
29, 34, 53, 54, 66, 90, 94, 104, 110, 111.

Keep us current
Information in travel guides is apt to change, which is why
we regularly update our guides. We'd be grateful to receive
feedback if you've noted something we should include in
our updates. If you have new information, please share
it with us by writing to the Commissioning Editor at the
MapStudio address on this page. The most significant
contribution to each new edition will receive a free copy of
the updated guide.

Front Cover: *Beach scene at sunset, near Holetown,
Barbados.*
Title Page: *King's Beach, fringed with coconut palms.*

917.2981
BA
ED. 4
2015

CONTENTS

1
Introducing Barbados

It seems at first like the shadow of a cloud on the waves, this isolated patch of land surrounded by nothing but sea as far as the horizon and beyond. It seems impossibly small and remote, but Barbados is a tiny island with great heart and indomitable spirit, comfortable within itself and genuinely happy to welcome the half a million visitors who flock to its shores each year. It is anything but politically correct, and the Barbadians are happy to explain why their gentle, confident, humorously cynical culture is so very different from other turbulent islands in the region.

'It is because the slave ships stopped here first. The best of the slaves were sold here, those who were conscientious and hardworking, who could use their brains and didn't make trouble. The ships then went on down the line until they reached Jamaica with only the aggressive troublemakers left on board Ɛ' They go on to extol the virtues of the 'motherland' (England) whose traditional ideals of democracy, freedom and fairness have been taken to heart, successfully put into practice and are still jealously guarded even though the younger generation tends to look more towards America's hamburger culture for inspiration. Above all, Barbados has developed its own distinctive national identity, confident enough to 'cherrypick' the best from elsewhere without losing its way.

Barbados is not perfect, but it is special, and not just for its golden sand and warm seas, its coral and turtles, the rum shops and reggae. The four cornerstones of Bajan life – Christianity, cricket, cooking and calypso –are all served

TOP ATTRACTIONS

*** **Swimming with turtles:** the boat trip of a lifetime.
*** **Submarine:** see the reef without a scuba tank.
*** **Oistins Fish Fry:** the place to be on a Friday night.
*** **Harrison's Cave:** spectacular limestone caves.
*** **Orchid World:** gardens dripping with exotic colour.
*** **Sunbury House:** fine old plantation home.
*** **Folkestone Marine Park:** protected coral reef, snorkelling, beach and picnic spot.

◀ *Opposite: Crane Bay, on the southeast coast of Barbados, is said by some to be one of the finest beaches in the Caribbean.*

INTRODUCING BARBADOS

FACT FILE

Geography: 430km² (166 sq miles); 34 x 22.5km (21 x 14 miles).
Population: 290,000 – of whom 93% are of African extraction, 3% European, 1% Indian/Asian and 3% mixed race.
Capital: Bridgetown.

with a laugh that shakes from the toes to the brain. Above all, from the rasta guys on the beach to sober-suited politicians and the church-going ladies with broad girths and big hats, the island's charm lives in its people.

THE LAND

Technically, this most famous of Caribbean islands is actually not a Caribbean island at all. Standing almost 160km (100 miles) east of the main archipelago, its western shores are gently caressed by the Caribbean, the eastern battered by Atlantic wind and waves.

Nor does it fit the mould physically. The main run of Caribbean islands is volcanic, the ridges and peaks of a huge underwater mountain range. Barbados, however, has just one small area of solid rock, in the northeast, forced upwards less than a million years ago by a vast seismic clash between the Atlantic and Caribbean tectonic plates. Most of the island is made of coral limestone that has gradually built up to a depth of about 90m (300ft). This means that the island is, quite literally, tilted, rising from the flat lands of the southwest, through the undulating hills of the

▶ *Right: There is little room to spare on this heavily populated island, with low-rise houses sprawling across every low hill.*

centre to the island's highest point at Mount Hillaby (340m/1115ft) and the dramatic 250m (800ft) cliffs overlooking the northeast coast. The capital, Bridgetown, in the southwest corner, is the only town of any size but houses still sprawl across most of the island. The only other towns that are anything more than a scattering of houses or ribbon development along the coasts are Holetown and Speightstown on the west coast and Bathsheba on the east.

▲ Above: Traditional houses are all built of wood with tin roofs; modern versions are often made of brick and concrete, styled to look like wood.

Water

There are no major rivers or lakes in Barbados. The country's only supply of fresh water is the rain that filters through the porous limestone, carving itself natural underground cisterns that store some of the world's purest water. Barbados is tiny, covering only 430km² (166 sq miles) – 34km x 22.5km (21 miles x 14 miles) – but it has a permanent population of around 267,000. When you add around a million tourists a year, half of them on day visits from cruise ships, the rest on longer holidays, it becomes one of the most densely populated countries in the world. The sheer volume of people, together with resource-hungry tourism projects from swimming pools to golf courses, mean that water is becoming ever more precious. By 2000, it was necessary to build the island's first desalination plant.

CLIMATE

For much of the year, the weather in Barbados is close to perfect – hot and sunny, with daytime temperatures of 24–35°C (75–95°F), and around 21–26°C (70–80°F) at night, with the sea water rarely below 25°C (78°F). Northeasterly trade winds keep the air fresh. January–June is the dry season. Hurricanes usually avoid the island, but there can be dramatic, short-lived tropical storms in July–September. Peak holiday season is December to April.

BARBADOS	J	F	M	A	M	J	J	A	S	O	N	D
AVERAGE TEMP. °C	24.5	24.5	24.5	26	27	27	26.5	27	27	26.5	26	25
AVERAGE TEMP. °F	76.5	76	77.5	79	80	80.5	80	80.5	80.5	79.5	79.5	77
RAINFALL mm	66	28	33	36	58	112	147	147	170	178	206	97
RAINFALL in	2.6	1.1	1.3	1.4	2.3	4.4	5.8	5.8	6.7	7.0	8.1	3.8

SUGAR

Sugar cane (*Saccharum officinarum*) was first cultivated in New Guinea in about 8000BC. By about 6000BC it was to be found in Indonesia, the Philippines and India, and by the 4th century BC – when Alexander the Great reached the subcontinent – the first fermented drinks were on offer. With the Islamic expansion of the 7th and 8th centuries AD, sugar reached Spain and Portugal and in their hands, some 800 years later, it jumped the Atlantic to the New World.

Vegetation

When the Europeans first arrived, the island was thickly forested with luxuriant species such as the bearded fig tree (said to have given the island its name – Portuguese for 'the bearded ones'), whitewood and West Indian cedar, while the white coral-sand beaches of the south and west coasts were interspersed by dense mangrove swamps. Today, with the island cleared over the centuries for building, cooking and sugar production, trees are scarce and only tiny pockets of fiercely guarded forest survive. Even then, the dominant tree within them is mahogany, introduced to the island in 1799 along with teak, a hardwood still prized for furniture manufacture. What hasn't already been built over is mainly blanketed by sugar-cane fields, although vegetables and fruit, from pawpaw (papaya) to breadfruit and bananas, are grown on a small scale, mainly in the north.

The country's British heritage is obvious in the flamboyant love of gardens that have lined the roads with vividly coloured flame trees, jacaranda and cascades of bougainvillea, while the centre of the island is home to several magnificent botanical gardens.

▼ *Below: Sugar cutting is hard work, especially in the midday heat.*

Wildlife

Isolated since the geological formation of the island, there is very little native wildlife in Barbados. Undoubtedly the most famous of its animals are the green monkeys, introduced by slaving ships from Senegal and Gambia about 350 years ago (*see* panel, page 88). Although there are thought to be up to 10,000 monkeys on the island, they are shy and it is difficult to catch more than a fleeting glimpse.

The largest of the local animals are the pigs, abandoned on the island in 1536 by Portuguese sailors and then left to run wild.

The largest common predator is the mongoose, introduced by the British from India in 1879 to deal with overenthusiastic snake and rodent populations. The problem was that mongooses are out and about during the day while rats are nocturnal, so while the snakes have gone, the rats (which introduced themselves, having hitch-hiked over on passing ships) are alive and well. Meantime the mongooses live mainly on ground-nesting birds – which have become increasingly rare as a result – and the occasional domestic chicken.

▲ *Above: Snowy egrets stalk the shallow mangrove swamps at Graeme Hall Nature Sanctuary.*

The indigenous black-bellied sheep looks like a cross between a sheep and goat and is ideally adapted to the tropical climate. You may also see hares, introduced for sport in the 1860s, red-footed tortoises, six species of bat (which account for twenty percent of all the island's mammals), various lizards, geckos and toads, while at night the whole island reverberates to the sound of tiny whistling tree frogs (*see* panel, page 64).

Able to commute without waiting for a passing ship, birds are more common, with around 214 species found here. The majority are migrants, such as ducks, ospreys, falcons, sandpipers, warblers and terns. About 40 species live permanently on the island. These include doves, pigeons, herons, egrets, blackbirds, hummingbirds and finches, as well as seven species of parrot, including budgerigars, parakeets and parrots.

Marine Life

In comparison with the paucity of land animals, the seas off Barbados are teeming with life in all shapes, sizes and colours. Tidal pools are alive with sea anemones, crabs and small fish such as grunts, squirrel and angelfish. Much of the west and south coasts are lined by barrier, fringe and patching coral reefs. They have suffered as a result of clumsy treatment, pollution, storm damage and bleaching by rising sea temperatures, but nevertheless provide for some spectacular diving and snorkelling. There are also around 200 shipwrecks, most lost accidentally, some deliberately sunk to create artificial reefs, of which 10 are regularly used for diving. The reefs are a magical landscape created by some 55 species of hard and soft corals, sea fans and sponges that are home to hundreds of fish, from huge moray eels and shimmering shoals of jacks to brightly coloured clown and parrot fish. Further offshore, commercial and sports fishermen alike are attracted by blue and white marlin, sailfish, yellowfin tuna, wahoo and dolphin fish or dorado (*see* panel, page 97). There are also various sea mammals, including bottlenose dolphins (year-round), sperm and humpback whales (March to May), but they are rarely seen in the immediate vicinity of the island.

The undoubted stars of the sea, how-ever, are the island's plentiful population of hawksbill turtles (*see* panel, page 108), which breed on the west-coast beaches, and are sufficiently habituated to humans to allow you to swim with them. Then, of course, there is the ubiquitous flying fish (*see* panel, page 28), seen more com-monly on the plate than swimming in the ocean. This fish is not only the national icon, but also its most popular food, served for breakfast, lunch and dinner.

▼ *Below: The flying fish, a wildlife phenomenon and feast all in one.*

HISTORY IN BRIEF

Bypassed by Columbus, and plundered but otherwise ignored by other Spanish sailors, Barbados's history is commonly considered to have started in 1536 when a Portuguese explorer, Pedro a Campos, dropped in long enough to give the island a name, *Los Barbudos* – 'the bearded ones' – after the forests of bearded fig trees. The island's prehistory, however, stretches back much further. Excavations during the building of Port St Charles in Speightstown uncovered evidence dating back to about 2000BC that the Tainos (Arawak), an Amerindian people, were living here at the time, eating flying fish and farming maize, cassava and sweet potatoes. Thought to have arrived from Venezuela in dugout canoes, they seem to have stayed, life relatively unchanged, for around 3000 years.

Later historic reports describe the Tainos as a short, olive-skinned people who bound their foreheads in infancy to create a sloping point and wore black and white body paint, cotton armbands, and nose plugs and rings of copper and gold alloys. They were farmers, who tended cotton, cassava, corn, peanuts, guavas, and pawpaws, and fished using nets, harpoons and hooks.

Their peaceful existence came to an abrupt end in about 1200 with the arrival of the taller, stronger and definitely more warlike Caribs, a people consistently accused of cannibalism. Gruesome stories tell of human barbecues served with cassava beer and even of the Caribs eating a whole French ship's crew in 1536. There is no reliable evidence to support this lurid mythology (*see* panel, this page) but they were undoubtedly extremely efficient bowmen who used poisoned arrows to fell their prey (human or animal).

Slaughtered by the Caribs, enslaved by the Spanish and with much of the rest of the population felled by the arrival of dreaded European diseases to which they had no

▼ Below: Pottery Tainos mask in the Barbados Museum, Bridgetown.

INTRODUCING BARBADOS

c. 1623BC The Tainos (Arawak) people, who are thought to have arrived in Barbados from Venezuela, are the first known human inhabitants of the island.

c. AD1200 The warlike Amerindian Carib people begin to visit the islands, preying on the Tainos people of Barbados.

1492 The Spanish arrive – and promptly start to enslave large numbers of the local population who are also decimated by European diseases such as smallpox and tuberculosis – but have no real interest in settling here permanently.

1536 Portuguese explorer Pedro a Campos visits the island, naming it *Los Barbudos* ('the bearded ones') after the bearded fig trees.

1625 The English arrive to find the island entirely abandoned by the Tainos and Caribs, with no human population remaining in Barbados. Captain John Powell claims the island for the Crown.

17 February 1627 The first colony is founded by Captain Henry Powell. Jamestown (now known as Holetown) is the first town to be established on the island.

1639 The islanders found the House of Assembly.

1630s–40s First sugar cane is grown on the island.

1651 Cromwell dispatches an army to subdue the royalist colony. As part of the terms of surrender, the Charter of Barbados guarantees a freely elected assembly and freedom from taxation without local consent. Cromwell begins the forced expatriation as 'indentured labour' of criminals, English and Scots royalist supporters and Irish rebels. It is estimated that up to 100,000 people were 'barbadosed'.

1654 Dutch Jews escaping from the Catholic Inquisition in Brazil introduce the art of sugar refining to the island and it becomes an instant bestseller, most of the sugar going to Holland on Dutch ships. The import of slaves from West Africa is geared up in order to work the new sugar plantations.

1663 Barbados becomes a British Crown possession.

1745–1830s Scots, who were dispossessed by the Highland Clearances, are also sent to the island as indentured servants.

1775 Rum replaces brandy as the official spirit ration of the British navy.

1780 British garrison established to fend off the French.

1807 Britain eventually bans the international trade in slaves.

1816 Slave revolt led by Bussa over misunderstood hopes of freedom.

1834 Slavery is officially abolished but the practice is, in effect, replaced by a compulsory 'apprentice' system in which labourers continue to work a 45-hour week with no pay.

1838 The apprentice system comes to an end, bringing a true end to slavery.

1843 Samuel Jackman Prescod becomes the first non-white member of the House of Assembly.

1876 The British propose a federation of Barbados and the Windward Islands, and this leads to bloody riots.

1924 Charles Duncan O'Neal forms a new political party, the Democratic League.

1938 Riots erupt due to economic poverty and depression. Grantley Adams founds the Barbados Labour Party (BLP).

1951 The start of universal adult suffrage. The Barbados Labour Party wins the general election.

1954 Ministerial government introduced, with Grantley Adams as the island's first prime minister.

1958–62 Short-lived West Indies Federation set up by the British, with Grantley Adams as prime minister.

1961 Barbados gets internal autonomy from Great Britain.

1966 Barbados gets full independence as a parliamentary democracy within the Commonwealth. The prime minister, Errol Walton Barrow, heads the government, while Queen Elizabeth II (of England) remains Head of State.

1973 The foundation of the Caribbean Community and Common Market (CARICOM).

◄ *Left: Sunbury is the largest and most elegant of the plantation homes open to the public, a world of privilege built on slave labour.*

natural immunity, the Tainos stood little chance. By the time the British arrived in 1625, the island was completely unin-habited, except for some wild pigs left by earlier sailors.

The Arrival of the British

Captain John Powell, a trader on his way home from Brazil, was the first Englishman to stop by, seizing the opportu-nity to run up the flag, claim the island in the name of King James I and name its first putative settlement Jamestown (unaware that the king had died while he was away). As soon as he got home, he reported back to his employer, Sir William Courteen, who immediately dispatched Captain Henry Powell (John's brother) to establish a settlement. His party of 80 settlers and 10 slaves arrived on 17 February 1627. Meanwhile, in London, the Earl of Marlborough leapt in ahead of Courteen's sponsor, the Earl of Montgomery, and succeeded in getting a royal patent to develop the fledg-ling colony, promptly making it over to the Earl of Carlisle. Bitter political recriminations resulted, both in London and Barbados, before Carlisle eventually won, leaving Courteen and his supporters out of pocket and extremely unhappy.

BLUNT ASSESSMENT

The Illand is the Dunghill wharone England doth cast forth its rubidg: Rodgs and hors and such like peopel are those which are generally Broght heare. A rodge in Engand will hardly make a cheater heare; a Baud brought over puts on a demuor comportment, a whore if hansum makes a wife for sume rich planter.

Henry Whistler, Journal,
9 February 1655

The Earl meanwhile happily handed out grants of land, and rich young men in search of a quick fortune flocked to the island. Amerindians from Guiana were recruited to help teach them survival techniques in the alien environment and labour was supplied in the form of indentured servants, people supposedly on a contract, but in effect slaves, who were transported in irons, bought and sold at auction. In the early years, these white slaves far outnumbered the black Africans. In 1701 records show that there were 21,700 white slaves on the island, known disparagingly as 'redlegs' and despised by the white landowners and black slaves alike.

Sugar and Slavery

The island's first cash crop was tobacco, but the market was soon flooded by product from Virginia. Other possible crops, such as indigo and ginger, were also tried, but success really only came when mainly Jewish Dutch settlers, expelled from Catholic Brazil, introduced plantation owners to the techniques of refining sugar cane. For the first few years it was used as fuel, animal feed and to make rum, but by the 1650s a lucrative transatlantic trade had built up, with sugar being exported to Holland.

The island was rapidly deforested to make way for cane fields, and plantation owners urgently sought a new supply of labour to tend their crops. They found it in West Africa.

▶ *Opposite: Sugar cane has been the island's life blood since the 1640s.*
▼ *Below: Rare early photographs give some idea of what life in the field would have been like for slave women.*

In 1629, there were only 50 black people on the island; by 1684, there were 46,502 and they made up 66% of the population. Of these, fewer than 100 were free men and women.

While the slave trade had been in existence for thousands of years before the Europeans became involved, and continued long after the trade was banned by the

British, the export of an estimated 10–20 million people to colonies throughout the world between the mid-17th century and 1807, and the appalling conditions they faced throughout their lives, is one of the most barbaric episodes in world history. Around 387,000 slaves are thought to have been brought to Barbados, which also acted as an entrepôt for the sale of slaves to America, Mexico, Venezuela and the other islands.

Cromwell

In 1639, the islanders formed a House of Assembly, which governed the colony together with an appointed council, the governor (representing the Crown) and the Anglican Church. Barbadians are proud of their status as the world's third oldest parliamentary 'democracy', but here – as elsewhere at the time – the vote was only available to white males of a certain social and financial standing. It was 1951 before all adults, regardless of sex or colour, finally received the vote.

The outbreak of civil war in England in 1640 brought the island's first real setbacks. Barbados remained, for the most part, loyal to the king. With his defeat, Parliament passed a punitive act prohibiting trade with the rebel islands. In 1651, the first Navigation Act made it illegal for the island to trade with any foreign power unless the goods were carried in British ships. That same year, Cromwell sent a naval expedition led by Sir George Ayscue to bring the colony into line. By January 1652, they were forced into submission, the terms enshrined in the Charter of Barbados, a surprisingly forward-thinking document that gave the island a freely elected assembly and freedom from taxation without local consent. With stability restored, Cromwell began to use the island as a dumping ground for undesirables, a practice continued after the restoration of the monarchy in 1660.

REDLEGS

In the mid-17th century, Cromwell used the 'redlegs' system to get rid of trouble-makers, whether criminal, religious or political. After the Monmouth Uprisings, the notorious 'hanging' Judge Jeffries 'barbadosed' 100 ringleaders, while thousands of Irish Catholics who objected to Cromwell's harsh form of Protestant rule were also clapped in irons. In 18th- and early 19th-century Scotland, English landowners fenced off what had once been common land, forcing many villagers from their homes, some being press-ganged into the navy, others forcibly transported to the colonies as indentured labour.

▲ *Above: Bussa breaks the shackles of slavery above a busy roundabout.*

TRAFFICKING

The African slaves brought to the Americas came mainly from West Africa, many of them from inland communities traded down to the Gold Coast (modern-day Ghana) by black and Arabic slavers who used the slave caravans as pack labour to carry ivory and gold from the interior. Most of those imported to Barbados were of the Asante, Ewe, Fon and Fante peoples, while some Yoruba, Efik, Igbo and Ibibio from present-day Nigeria were also enslaved.

As the population rose and the island became one of the most densely populated of the colonies, its people spread out to Jamaica, Cuba and South Carolina to help establish other societies.

As the 17th century drew to a close, the planters began to feel the pressure from competition in Guadeloupe and Martinique, but the early 18th century was, in the main, a period of stability. In the 1760s politics halfway across the world began to encroach again. The American War of Independence cut off the lucrative North American rum and molasses markets, while the Napoleonic Wars in Europe left the island vulnerable to attack by the French. This was countered by the arrival of the first Barbados garrison in 1780, followed by a resident naval force. The French never did attack and Barbados has the singular distinction of being the only Caribbean island to remain under one flag from colonization to independence.

Emancipation

In 1761, Quakers in England began their campaign for the abolition of slavery, and in 1772, the Chief Justice, Lord Mansfield, made a landmark judgement that the state of slavery could not exist in England. It was a catalyst for the antislavery movement, led by Samuel Wilberforce. With attention focused on Napoleon, however, it was 1807 before the British Parliament abolished the slave trade. In Barbados, the plantation owners supported the move. By this stage, with a large population of slave women, the island was self-sufficient in slave babies and would have a distinct commercial advantage when the other sugar islands lost their labour supply. But when it came to abolishing slavery itself, things were very different, and the landowners fought a fierce rearguard action to protect their 'property'. The slaves, prompted by rumours of coming change, became restless and after several skirmishes, in 1816, a full-scale rebellion was launched, led by Bussa, an African-born man now regarded as one of the heroes of emancipation. Although the revolt was short-lived, it was extremely bloody, with nearly 1000 slaves killed and 140 executed before it was over.

In 1826, the Barbados government reluctantly passed legislation improving the living and working conditions of slaves and finally, in 1834, slavery was officially abolished. However, it was replaced by an apprenticeship system that bound slaves to continue working for their masters. In 1938, this too was abolished and 70,000 men, women and children took to the streets in celebration, free at last. Even then, few had any options other than to stay on the plantations as they had no money, no land and no other home. Their 'house-spot' was rented in exchange for their labour. The chattel house was born as workers found a way to pack all their belongings, including the house itself, and move to a new location.

A REASON TO SING

Lick and Lock-up done wid,
Hurrah fuh Jin-Jin;
Lick and Lock-up done wid,
Hurrah fuh Jin-Jin.

God bless de Queen
fuh set we free,
Hurrah fuh Jin-Jin;
Lick and Lock-up done wid,
Hurrah fuh Jin-Jin

1833 Barbadian folk song celebrating the end of slavery [Jin-Jin is Victoria, licking is whipping, lock-up the jail]

▼ Below: This drawing in the Barbados Museum shows the people taking to the island's streets to celebrate emancipation.

Good Times, Bad Times

Slowly things began to improve. The island had always had good schools and these were now opened to all, while the churches made a concerted effort to 'civilize' the former slaves. Samuel Jackman Prescod, son of a white father and slave mother, was one of the great inspirations of the age, and in 1843 he became the first non-white member of the House of Assembly.

In 1840, a regular steamship connected Barbados with England, and in 1872 the island received its first telegram via submarine cable. Amongst the other miracles of modern technology established in Barbados were gasworks, a public water supply, telephone service and a railway between Bridgetown and Belleplaine in St Andrew (axed in 1937 – *see* panel, page 71).

In 1796, Captain Bligh (of *The Bounty* fame) introduced a new species of sugar cane with a far higher yield. Improvements in farming techniques, such as the use of fertilizer and selective breeding of new strains, also saw massive increases in sugar production. The island had its first steam-driven mill in 1850, and by 1900 there were a hundred peppering the landscape.

With the turn of the century, life became harder again. European sugar beet was now a cheaper competitor, war in Europe damaged supply and it began to look as if the sweet times were gone. A terrible hurricane in 1898 was followed by an outbreak of smallpox in 1902. From 1904 to 1914, some 20,000 Bajans headed to Panama to build the canal. Others moved to Brazil, Cuba and other nearby countries in search of work. With the plantation owners deep in debt, labourers were finally able to buy their own plots of land. The British government invested

▼ *Below: Huge combine harvesters cut the cane these days; only hard-to-reach gullies are still slashed by hand.*

thousands of pounds in propping up the sugar industry. In 1951, the Commonwealth Sugar Agreement gave Barbados protected access to markets and in 1975 this was rolled into a generous European Union quota. This ended in 2006, however, and the island, now forced to fend for itself, is looking for other ways to make a living. Possibilities include sugar production for conversion to biodegradable plastics and ethanol (bio-fuel).

Independence

Barbados had always enjoyed a far greater degree of independence than most of the colonies. A proposal, in 1876, that the island join the Windward Islands as a federal Crown colony was met by riots. Change was inevitable, however, and as the sugar barons struggled in the early 20th century, black Barbadians, with their new-won education and property, began to demand more of a say. In 1924, a local doctor and social reformer, Charles Duncan O'Neal, formed the Democratic League, the island's first populist political party. The following year came the first trade union, the Workingmen's Association. From these grew both the Barbados Labour Party (1938) and the Barbados Workers' Union (1941).

People were also listening hard to the back-to-Africa messages of Jamaican Marcus Garvey and Trinidadian Clement Payne. When Payne was deported in 1937, rioting broke out. Out of the upheaval came a new popular leader, Grantley Adams, who founded a political coalition, the Barbados Progressive League. It gained its first seats in 1940, and in 1942 changes to the political system gave women the vote and made Adams leader of the House.

In 1958, a second attempt was made at federalizing the West Indies with Grantley Adams at its helm. This, too, failed in 1962 and Adams lost power in 1961 to Errol Walton Barrow and his Democratic Labour Party. It was Barrow who led the country to full independence in 1966 and served as its first independent prime minister.

CLEMENT PAYNE

Born in Trinidad in 1904, Clement Osbourne Payne is one of the island's official national heroes. His actions finally came to a head in 1937 when he held public meetings across Barbados, denouncing living conditions and urging workers to create militant communities to resist the white planters, using the slogan 'Educate, agitate, but do not violate!' Arrested on the pretext of immigration violations, he was deported from Barbados, leading to mass violence that left 14 dead, 47 wounded and 500 arrested. The resulting Moyne Commission upheld many of Payne's complaints and introduced trade unions to the island. Payne himself died in 1941, having never set foot on Barbados again.

INTRODUCING BARBADOS

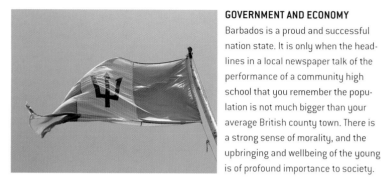

▲ *Above: Blue on blue – the Barbadian flag flies over National Heroes Square in Bridgetown.*

GOVERNMENT AND ECONOMY

Barbados is a proud and successful nation state. It is only when the headlines in a local newspaper talk of the performance of a community high school that you remember the population is not much bigger than your average British county town. There is a strong sense of morality, and the upbringing and wellbeing of the young is of profound importance to society.

Parliament

Constitutionally, Barbados is a parliamentary democracy based on the British model. Parliament consists of a 30-seat House of Assembly, elected by the public, and a 21-member Senate appointed by the Governor General. Elections are held every five years. The Head of State is Queen Elizabeth II, represented on the island by Governor General Sir Elliot Fitzroy Belgrave. Prime Minister Freundel Stuart is leader of the Democratic Labor Party, which retained a narrow majority in the 2013 elections. At a local level, the country is divided into 11 parishes, each historically centred on an Anglican church.

Economy

Until recently the country's economy remained heavily based on sugar and its by-products, with tourism coming a strong second. However, with the ending of the protected sugar quotas, the market imploded and the government had to work hard to develop new forms of income such as financial and business services and manufacturing – the latter hampered by the island's lack of natural resources and high transport costs. They have been remarkably successful with over three-quarters of the island's GDP now coming from the service industries.

Efforts are also being made to diversify agriculture and make the island more self-reliant – at the moment, virtually all

THE FLAG

The national flag of Barbados has three equal vertical panels, two of ultramarine, representing the sea and sky of Barbados, flanking a centre panel of gold representing the island's sandy beaches. A black trident in the centre symbolizes Neptune, the mythical god of the sea, its broken shaft marking the break with Britain.

food is imported. The country is facing a difficult task but success can be seen everywhere, in the new buildings, the relatively affluent lifestyle of most of its people, and in the fact that the UN recently rated it as one of the top 10 developing nations.

This also comes with its own problems, such as over-enthusiastic economic migration from other, less successful Caribbean countries, overdevelopment and a lack of water on a very crowded island, inflated property prices and limited access to public beaches as more and more up-market tourism developments line the coast and try to keep the beach exclusive to their guests.

Above all, the islanders are justly proud of their record in education, topping the poll worldwide with an effective 100% literacy rate. Bridgetown is home to one of the largest campuses of the multinational University of the West Indies and many young people travel abroad for further education or work experience.

In 1965, Barbados was a founder member of the Caribbean Free Trade Association (CARIFTA), which was commuted in 1975 into CARICOM – the Caribbean Community and Common Market. Fifteen countries are now members of this economic free trade area, with five associate members. Links between members are growing, with the West Indies cricket team and the University of the West Indies the most high profile of many common projects. CARICOM, like the EU, is growing ever closer to a single political and economic entity and may well eventually prove to be the basis for a third attempt at a federal system. Meantime, CARICOM and the EU have signed a joint Economic Partnership Agreement, which is being used as a major step towards a single market within the Caribbean. Culturally, people are being encouraged to see themselves first as West Indian, then as Bajan, on the basis that narrowly focused nationalism will not lead to success for any country in the region.

GRANTLEY ADAMS

Officially a national hero, with his picture on the B$100 note, and the airport named after him, Sir Grantley Herbert Adams (1898–1971) was the son of a local headmaster. He studied in Oxford and practised as a barrister before entering parliament in 1934. In 1938 he became vice president of the newly formed Barbados Labour Party and became its leader in 1939. In 1941 he was also elected president of the Barbados Workers' Union. In 1942 he joined the Governor's Executive Committee. In 1954 he became the island's first premier. He was knighted in 1957 and the following year became prime minister of the short-lived Federation of the West Indies.

▼ *Below: Up-market tourist developments try to keep the beaches exclusive to their guests.*

Body and Soul

It is easy to see what matters to the Bajans. This tiny community has an astonishing 365 churches – one for every day of the year. Even more telling, there are over 1600 rum shops on the island, many of them situated conveniently near the churches! Together the spiritual and the spirits fuel much of the island's community spirit.

▼ *Below: The Anglican Church of St Mary in the capital, Bridgetown.*

THE PEOPLE

Although geographically isolated, the people of Barbados are anything but insular. Linked by a common heritage both to the rest of the Caribbean and the rest of the Commonwealth, over the years many have gone abroad to work or study – in Panama, Canada, the United Kingdom and elsewhere. Then there are the million tourists who visit their shores each year, satellite TV and radio, as well as an astonishingly active news media for such a small population.

Religion

God definitely rules here, with even most of the younger people worshipping regularly and over 100 religions represented on the island. During the British period, the Anglican Church was dominant, the whole fabric of the island structured into parishes, each centred on an Anglican church. On abolition, most of the slaves adopted the religion of their former masters and nearly a third of Bajans remain Anglican today (still a significant majority, but down from 90% in 1871). Many other Christian churches, however, have a strong presence on the island. The Quakers were one of the main forces behind abolition, long before anyone else was talking about it, upsetting the authorities to such an extent that in 1676 a law was passed forbidding black people to attend Quaker meetings. That law was only repealed in 1810. The Moravians fared better when they arrived in 1765 to evangelize the slaves, but the Methodists who followed them in 1789 so angered the white

◄ *Left: St John's Church on the east coast is a classic neo-Gothic English design.*

Barbadians that a mob destroyed the James Street Chapel in 1823. Both denominations now flourish, with thousands of adherents.

The Catholics have four churches and about 4% of the population, but the greatest shift is towards a wide array of newer evangelical faiths with more radical views and better music. The Spiritual Baptist Church, founded by Archbishop Granville Williams, arrived from Trinidad in 1957, its 10,000 followers wearing brightly coloured headscarves (giving them their local nickname, 'tie-heads'), practising total immersion baptism in the sea and worshipping in an energetic Afro-centric style with drumming, music and dance.

In addition to all these Christian churches, there are a few Muslims and a long-settled but tiny community of Jews. About 300 of them, persecuted by the Dutch, fled from Recife in Brazil in the mid-17th century, bringing with them knowledge of sugar-cane production and so transforming the island.

Probably the last of the significant religions introduced to the island was Rastafarianism, its followers highly visible with their dreadlocks (said to resemble the lion's mane) and red, yellow and green crocheted hats (the colours of the

RASTA MAN

Based on the black power teachings of Marcus Garvey in the 1920s, Rastafarianism, which originated in Jamaica, focused on Ras Tafari, who was crowned Emperor Haile Selassie I of Ethiopia in 1930. Claiming a direct lineage back to David, Solomon and Sheba, Ras Tafari was proclaimed 'King of Kings, Lord of Lords, and the conquering lion of the tribe of Judah' and was seen as a Messiah.

Above all, he was black and the religion founded around him, which draws on both Jewish and Christian traditions, embraces the idea of black liberation from oppression.

INTRODUCING BARBADOS

OBEAH

Although obeah does contain elements of witchcraft, in most other respects it is similar to other African religions, with the ancestors providing a conduit to God, and the obeah-man a central figure in the community – priest, healer, and counsellor. Obeah is not devil worship and does not raise the dead, but it is held by its followers to have potent magical power.

Ethiopian flag). With a largely young following, the rastas soon gained a reputation as loud, dangerous drug addicts, but true followers believe in peace, live a simple life, abstain from alcohol, and avoid business dealings.

Few Bajans are true adherents, but many believe in the power of obeah, a form of African spiritualism similar to voodoo, which was one of the main forms of worship among the slaves. Used as a potent force for good or evil, it is thought to hold the power to produce results from the death or disgrace of an enemy to love potions that will get you your man. In times of decision or crisis, some Barbadians choose a belt-and-braces approach, praying in church but still visiting the 'obeah-man'. Obeah is illegal on the island.

Music

Bajans love music, but have no purely home-grown forms, and instead import and adapt music from across the world. You can find classical music, including a symphony orchestra, chamber music ensemble and festival choir, as well as choral church music. The annual **Holders Festival** brings in world-class music, opera and drama, while the **Jazz Festival** also attracts big-name acts for concerts such as the massive **Reggae on the Hill** at Farley Park, which brings out up to 20,000 fans. The many local churches provide a stunning range of gospel choirs, while May sees them in full voice for the Caribbean's biggest Gospel Festival. The island has a staggering nine recording studios, five of them serious players attracting international stars including the Rolling Stones, Sting and Eddie Grant, who runs his Ice Label from here.

Calypso is the most famous of the Caribbean creations, dating back to 18th-century Trinidad. Also known as *kaiso*, its roots are a potent mix of African, French, British,

▼Below: The Jazz Festival is one of the highlights of the Barbadian calendar.

Spanish and Indian influences while the lyrics mix satire, social commentary and conscience and political polemic. Many will be incomprehensible to visitors, but ask a local for a translation and you can find yourself tapped into a gleefully scandalous version of local happenings. Recently, 'rapso' has begun to fuse calypso and rap (both fulfilling the same social purpose for different groups and ages), while 'chutney' is an (east) Indian variation.

Soca is a 20th-century invention, a compelling calypso-based dance music that adds a heavy percussion backing to the musical mix and has taken over as the sound of choice. Then there is 'chutney-soca', not to forget 'ragga-soca' (mixing reggae and soca) ... Drumming was outlawed by the British in 1883 as dangerously subversive but people with music in their soul always find a way to express themselves. In Trinidad, *tamboo-bamboo* bands used anything they could find, with tuneable bamboo sticks, dustbin lids and old cooking pans. Even when it became legal again, few had the money for proper instruments, but carnival required complexity and anything from tin cans to biscuit tins were added to the mix before a drummer named

▲ *Above: A steel band like this one in Bridgetown will have up to eight drummers who all take years to learn their skill.*

THE BEAT GOES ON

Star performers of calypso and soca include the late Lord Shorty, The Mighty Gabby, The Mighty Sparrow, Krosfyah (led by singer-songwriter Edwin Yearwood), Mac Fingall, The Merrymen, Square One (with frontwoman Alison Hinds) and Red Plastic Bag, while internationally famous soca songs include *Hot, Hot, Hot* and *Who Let the Dogs Out?* In Barbados, leading reggae artists include David Kirton, Biggie Irie and jazz saxophonist Arturo Tappin.

INTRODUCING BARBADOS

▶ *Right: The steel pan started as an illegal form of expression, but has become a highly tuned precision instrument.*

Winston 'Spree' Simon created the tuned tin in 1939. During World War II, the musical possibilities of oil drums were discovered and the steel band was born. These days, the sound has grown up and **steel pans** have become precision instruments, with 32 notes, major and minor keys, that take skilled craftsmen weeks to hone to perfect pitch. A modern band will have 10 pans, giving it the tonal spread of a grand piano.

In more recent years, Jamaica has proved to be the overriding inspiration in the development of new musical forms coming out of the Caribbean. Like other local creations, **reggae** has its roots in African drumming and the slave plantations, but this variation, which first came to life as 'ska' during the run-up to the island's independence in the late 1950s, is slower, more concerned with rhythm than melody. Reggae was also the first of the Caribbean musical forms to become truly international, taken around the world in the 1970s by musical giants such as Bob Marley and the Wailers, who also gave it its close definition with Rastafarianism. From reggae were born dub, remix, hip hop and many of the other musical forms that dominate popular music today, whether created by musicians or star DJs.

TUK IN

Landship players parody military drill, the British tradition and life at sea with jigs, hornpipes and maypole dances, waltzes and military marches to the African beat of *tuk*. This drum-based musical tradition flourished on the 17th-century slave plantations until it was banned as the owners suspected the drumming contained covert messages. Legalized after emancipation, it borrowed heavily from the British military tradition, its instruments including kettle and bass drums and the penny whistle.

Music on the Move

The extraordinary **Barbadian Landship Movement** – founded in 1837 by a retired seaman, Moses Wood – models itself on the Royal Navy but in spite of being surrounded by water, the 'ship' never goes near a real boat, being based instead at a 'dock' (wooden house). Male members wear naval bellbottoms, the women dress as naval nurses, while the ship's leaders are known as admiral, captain, bo'sun and so on. The members actually also undergo a measure of naval training, and perform a much bigger social function, offering service and support to charities across the island, but they are undoubtedly best known as entertainers, comedians and musicians.

Although there are festivals and holidays through the year (*see* page 125), the island explodes during Crop Over (twelve weeks from June to August), traditionally the harvest festival at the end of the sugar-cutting season, re-established as a major tourist attraction in 1974. Travelling colourful landship crews and *tuk* bands wander the island, trailing dancers in their wake. Celebrations also include a donkey-cart parade, a King and Queen of the Crop competition and the 'Pic-o-de-Crop' Calypso Monarch competition – and everywhere are those Bajan staples, both music and rum.

▼ *Below: The Kadooment Day Parade is a glorious Caribbean carnival.*

INTRODUCING BARBADOS

Food

On this tiny island, far distant from any other land, most food is imported, so you can get almost anything as long as you are prepared to pay. Food is plentiful, varied and excellent, but not cheap. However, the traditional local diet is far more constrained, a relatively small range of ingredients souped up by mind-blastingly, tongue-numbingly hot pepper sauce. Fish is the main source of protein. Flying fish (*see* panel, this page) are ubiquitous, but game fish such as dolphin fish (dorado), tuna and barracuda are also common. These are baked, grilled, fried, stewed and turned into salt fish balls and fish cakes. Shellfish, from spiny lobsters to sea urchins, are now in dangerously short supply and are rarities or even, in some cases, banned.

Meat of all sorts is on the menu, but look out for the local black-bellied lamb (halfway between a sheep and a goat). Most common is pork, every part of the pig from trotters to ears fetching up on the plate in some form or other, from the Sunday roast joint, with lime and salt crackling, to a very local speciality, pudding and *souse*. Pudding is grated sweet potato in a pig's intestine, seasoned and steamed. *Souse* is the meat from the head and feet, cooked long and slow and pickled with lime, onion, salt, cucumber and parsley. Also look out for the fancifully named *cohobblopot*, a highly spiced meat and okra stew.

▶ Right: Captain Bligh looked after his breadfruit trees so well that his crew mutinied. For Barbadians at least, Bligh had his priorities right.

Sweet potato is only one of many carbohydrates borrowed freely from other cultures, with bread and potatoes, yams, maize, plantains, breadfruit (introduced from Tahiti by Captain Bligh in 1793), cassava and rice all on the menu. Staple local dishes include African-style *cou-cou* (*see* panel, this page), Caribbean rice and peas (pulses such as black beans), and old-fashioned British macaroni pie – macaroni with a cheese sauce, baked in the oven.

If you fancy a snack, a cutter is a sandwich, while a *roti* is hugely filling Indian-style flat bread stuffed with curry. Desserts, on the other hand, tend to owe more to the British nursery than any exotic influence, with options from bread-and-butter pudding to treacle tart and jelly (jello) lined up on the buffet. For a healthier option, select from the fabulous array of local fruit, including Barbadian cherries and grapefruit, created on the island in the 18th century by crossing a sweet orange with a bitter Polynesian shaddock.

Wash it all down with the local water, with or without a splash of fresh lime, coconut water sipped direct from the nut, Banks beer or, of course, rum punch (*see* panel, page 58).

▲ *Above: The water's edge of Bridgetown harbour is lined with a number of bustling bistros, cafés and restaurants.*

Cou-cou

Closely related to Ghanaian *foo-foo*, *cou-cou* is a stiff maize meal porridge, cooked with okra reduced to a liquid mush. The final porridge should be stiff enough to come away from the sides of the pan. Originally designed to fill the stomach quickly and cheaply, it is a bland starch, usually served with meat and gravy or salt fish. Similar porridges are made from bread-fruit, plantains, yams and potatoes.

2
Bridgetown

When the British first arrived in 1627, they settled in Jamestown (now Holetown) on the west coast, but it proved less than ideal and a year later they found a more suitable place for a town next to a sheltered inlet in Carlisle Bay on the south coast. Safe anchorage for their ships and easy land for building outweighed the risk of fever in the low-lying mangrove swamps and woods. The Earl of Carlisle granted 100 acres of land to the Syndicate of London Merchants. At first, they named their new town Indian Bridge, after the rudimentary bridge that had been slung across the Careenage by the Indians. As the country began to sort itself out into parishes, it became known for a while as St Michael, but in 1654, when the new bridge across the Careenage was built, the town finally settled on the name Bridgetown.

The early town was a rough-and-ready place with many taverns, prostitutes and even visiting pirates. Of 1650 Bridgetown, Richard Ligon said, '... a town so ill situate for if they had considered health, as they did convenience, they would never have set it there ...' Within 50 years, however, it had been transformed into a model of respectability. According to Father Labat, who visited in 1700, '... the whole has an air of neatness, politeness and opulence ...'

Today, the swamps have long gone, the main docks have moved out of town and the city has since burst its boundaries to spread over the whole southwestern corner of Barbados. 'Greater' Bridgetown now has a population of about 110,000, while many more commute here to work. The original street plan still exists and there are a few old

DON'T MISS

*** **The Careenage:** waterfront walkways and cafés.
*** **Broad Street:** vibrant shopping centre of Barbados.
*** **St Michael's Cathedral:** impressive Anglican place of worship.
*** **Pelican Village:** eat, drink and spend money.
*** **Nidhe Israel Synagogue:** the oldest synagogue in the western hemisphere.

◄ *Opposite: National Heroes Square has a statue of Nelson and a car park, but may, one day, celebrate the ten official national heroes of Barbados.*

31

BRIDGETOWN

▲ *Above: The low-lying lights of Bridgetown at night from the sea.*

buildings, but they are rare. Over the years, there have been three major hurricanes and 11 huge fires, all of which ran rampant through the closely packed wooden structures. Most of the historic architecture postdates the hurricane of 1831 and the last major fire in 1910. Nevertheless, it is a charismatic city, bustling with life and well worth exploring. The air of opulence remains, helped by cruise passengers streaming off the ships eager to shop, and by the increasing presence of mirror-glass office blocks filled with international companies taking advantage of tax breaks and skilled staff.

CENTRAL BRIDGETOWN

A day should be plenty to see the main sights. Those in the city centre are all within easy walking distance of National Heroes Square.

National Heroes Square

Barbados has 10 national heroes, the list published on 28 April 1998, the centenary of the birth of Sir Grantley Adams (*see* panel, page 21). However, the city's main square, between the waterfront and Houses of Parliament, began life as Trafalgar Square in honour of the great naval battle of 1805 in which Nelson soundly trounced Napoleon, losing his life in the process. The name was changed in 1999, but in spite of this, **National Heroes Square** bears no memorials or

NELSON IN BARBADOS

Lord Horatio Nelson (1758–1805), Britain's greatest naval hero, spent less than 24 hours anchored in Carlisle Bay on his only visit to Barbados, but the planters felt that his presence in the area had been sufficient to save them from the French and raised a statue after his death at Trafalgar. A local threat still offers to 'show you de ball dat shoot Nelson'.

statues to the 10. Instead there's a statue of Nelson by Richard Westmacott, erected in 1813 – well ahead of the one in London (1849).

Within 20 years, people were campaigning to have Nelson's statue removed, while in 1908, Frederick Treves described it as 'not impressive, while the famous mariner is make to look bored and jaundiced'. The clamour to replace it with true Bajan heroes is now strong and will almost certainly prevail. For the moment, however, both Nelson and his attendant pigeons remain in place, surrounded by a car park and taxi rank. Nelson's pedestal is the island's official Point 0, against which all distances on the island are measured. The area is used for official celebrations and Christmas carol concerts.

At the far end of the square, the **Cenotaph** is the national war memorial, erected in 1925 to honour the Barbadian dead of World War I. The names of those who died during World War II were added in 1953. Next to it,

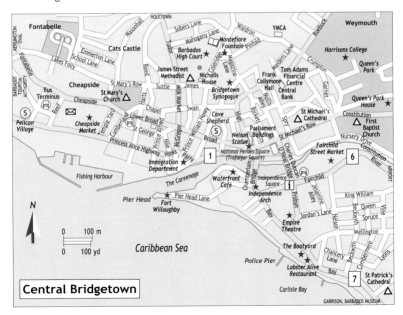

Central Bridgetown

the **Dolphin Fountain and Gardens** (1865) celebrate the arrival of piped running water to the island in 1861. Ironically, as water is now so scarce on the island, the fountain never plays.

Parliament Buildings

Behind National Heroes Square, the castle-like grey coral limestone buildings with jalousie windows are the **Parliament Buildings**.

Barbados is proud of its reputation as the third oldest parliament within the Commonwealth (after Bermuda and Britain). Its parliament was founded in 1639, and it is thought that the first meeting was held in an upstairs room of a tavern adjacent to the site of the Central Bank of Barbados (Tom Adams Financial Centre); a commemorative monument, dedicated on 26 June 1989, stands at the corner of Spry and Roebuck streets. For centuries, members continued to meet in taverns, public buildings and even private homes before they finally decided to build themselves a home in the mid-19th century. The offices eventually opened for business in 1872, with the Assembly following in 1873. In the debating chamber, stained-glass windows represent all the British monarchs from James I to Queen Victoria — and Cromwell. It is only possible to see inside when the House is in session, when you may watch from the public gallery if suitably dressed.

The clock and peal of bells was added in 1884, and moved to its present position in 1886. The pendulum is 4m (14ft) long and the copper dials 2m (7ft) in diameter.

The Careenage

Also next to the square, the **Careenage** is the city's old inner harbour. It was this calm river mouth, with its shallow sloping shore, ideal for loading ships, that made the British

A Union Man

Charles Duncan O'Neal (1879–1936), one of the island's 10 national heroes, studied medicine in Edinburgh and served as a local councillor in Sunderland before returning to the Caribbean. In 1924, he finally returned to Barbados, where he became a vociferous social reformer, and a founder member of both the Workingmen's Association and the Democratic League. He entered Parliament in 1932. His portrait is on the B$10 bill.

first choose to settle here. Gradually as the harbour grew busier and boats were brought out of the water to be careened (scraped clear of barnacles) and repainted, it took on its current name. In later years, the inlet was deepened to allow larger vessels, but these days the Careenage is used only by pleasure boats – some private, some fishing charters and smaller tour boats.

Two bridges cross the water from National Heroes Square. The larger modern bridge on the left is **Charles Duncan O'Neal Bridge**, named after the great social reformer (*see* panel, page 34). The more decorative humpbacked bridge straight ahead is **Chamberlain Bridge**, rebuilt in place of the original swing bridge after the Great Hurricane in 1898. It was named after British Colonial Secretary Joseph Chamberlain (1836–1914) in thanks to the British for their generosity in helping the island to recover from the devastating effects of the hurricane. It was an early forerunner of this bridge that gave the town its name. The **Independence Arch** was erected during the 21st anniversary celebrations of Barbadian independence in 1987.

On the far side, the Lewis-Wickham Boardwalk has an attractive range of shops and cafés, including the excellent Waterfront Café (*see* page 116) and is an ideal place to stop for lunch during a hard day's sightseeing and shopping.

TRAVELLER'S TALES

Richard Ligon, an escaped royalist, fled to Barbados in 1647, returning to England three years later. His stories so enraptured his friends that he was persuaded to publish an account of his adventures. *A True & Exact History of the Island of Barbados*, published in 1657, gives us one of the most detailed and colourful accounts of life in the early years of the colony.

◀ *Opposite: The splendid Victorian Parliament Buildings look more like a Gothic cathedral than the seat of government.*
▼ *Below: National Heroes Square and Parliament from the Careenage, the first harbour to be built in Bridgetown.*

The Pier Head

At the tip of the peninsula dividing the Careenage from the open sea, the **Pier Head** was built to allow larger ships to dock, but relentless progress resulted in the creation of the Deep Water Harbour, leaving this former port derelict. Today, the Pier Head, site of the world's only surviving screw lifting dock, is supposedly being redeveloped after years of neglect, although plans are years behind and mired in controversy. At its tip, **Fort Willoughby** cost 36,300kg (80,000lb) of sugar to build in 1656, and was named after the then governor, Francis Willoughby, the Fifth Baron Willoughby of Parham. The fort, long used by the national coastguard and the navy, is supposedly to be redeveloped as a naval heritage centre.

Walk back along the south side of the Careenage through **Independence Square**, now more a car park than a place of celebration. Behind it, **Fairchild Street** — named after the Chief Justice in 1752 — was one of the roughest in town, a centre of prostitution and breeding ground of the cholera epidemic of 1854, which killed 20,727 people before it burned itself out. Head past the main bus station and you reach **Fairchild Street Market**, one of two large daily markets in Bridgetown, a loud, brightly coloured, photogenic bustle of activity.

▼ *Below: Independence Arch, built in 1987 to commemorate 21 years of independence, shows all the island's national symbols — the coat of arms, flying fish, pelican, pride of Barbados flower and bearded fig tree.*

St Michael's Cathedral

Cross back over the Charles Duncan O'Neal Bridge and turn right onto St Michael's Row. One block on, you reach St Michael's Cathedral. The first Church of St Michael was a puny affair constructed in 1641. By 1665, it was obviously inadequate and land was donated for a larger stone church. This did sterling service until it was destroyed by a hurricane in 1780. The islanders held a lottery, which raised £10,000, allowing them to build a new, even grander church that was able to accommodate up to 3000, with a solidly imposing tower and peal of bells. It was the largest in the Americas, a fitting place to become a cathedral when Bishop William Hart Coleridge arrived in 1825, one of the first two bishops in the Caribbean (the other was in Jamaica).

▲ *Above: St Michael's Cathedral, funded by a lottery as the home of one of the first bishoprics in the Caribbean.*

Although again damaged by a hurricane in 1831, the basic plan of the church remains much as it was in the 18th century, with the cathedral chapter added in 1888 and the Chapel of the Blessed Sacrament in 1938. It is simple and classical in style, built of coral stone with a gallery on three sides and imposing stained-glass windows. Inside, take a look at the barrel-vaulted ceiling, built as an upturned boat; the pipe organ, considered to be one of the best in the western hemisphere; the small marble font, dated 1680; the carved mahogany pulpit and choir stalls; and a fascinating collection of tombstones and memorial tablets. Several former governors, as well as Grantley and Tom Adams, are buried here. The bells, sadly, no long ring. Open daily 09:00–16:00, tel: 427 0790, www.saintmichaelscathedral.bb

Two blocks to the north, the 11-storey **Tom Adams Financial Centre**, Spry Street, is the tallest building on the island, home to the Central Bank and the island's only fully fledged concert hall, the **Frank Collymore Hall** [tel: 436 9083/4, www.fch.org.bb].

AMEN TO ALL THAT

Amen Alley, opposite St Michael's Cathedral, is where black people would congregate during services. Banned from sitting inside the cathedral with the white worshippers, they would wait patiently until it was time to say Amen at the end of the service.

Take your passport and travel ticket with you when you shop because they are your passport to significant savings on everything, from clothes to cameras, at the many duty-free shops on the island. You may take some things away with you but others, such as alcohol, tobacco and electronics, will be delivered to the airport or cruise terminal for you to pick up on departure.

Broad Street

Return to National Heroes Square and leave it in the opposite direction along the rather ironically named **Broad Street**. Originally named Cheapside when it was laid out in 1657, it was reserved for 'a market place and other public uses'. The name changed a couple of times, to Exchange Street and then New England Street, before it finally settled as Broad Street by 1703 when the name first appeared in print. Its use, however, never varied and it is still the main shopping street on the island – Oxford Street and Fifth Avenue rolled into one – with department stores and duty-free outlets vying for space with fashion and souvenir shops and corporate offices. Architecturally it is a total mishmash, based on traditional two-storey houses with overhanging balconies, but look up above the shop signs for everything from Victorian gingerbread to 1960s glass, sometimes on the same building!

Cave Shepherd is the country's largest department store, while the Da Costa Mall is home to over 35 shops. There are also plenty of jewellery outlets for those who want to take advantage of the duty-free prices.

CHEAPSIDE

As the road heads west, it becomes poorer, changes into Lower Broad Street and eventually reverts to its original name, Cheapside. On the right, **St Mary's Church** stands on the site of the original Church of St Michael (*see page 37*). St Mary's, built in 1827 to house the overflow from St Michael's Cathedral, is an elegant Georgian affair that doubles as a hurricane shelter. The tower is a later addition. The church is built on a burial ground originally reserved for the city's non-white population,

◀ Left: Pelican Village has an array of craft and souvenir shops in reproduction chattel houses.

◀◀ Opposite: Broad Street is surprisingly narrow, but is a busy hub, with porcelain, potatoes, pepper sauce and petticoats all on sale.

while the large silk cotton tree in the grounds, known as the Justice Tree, was the site of public hangings. Perhaps unsurprisingly, the church has had a long history of involvement with political activism. Among those now buried in the shady churchyard is Samuel Jackman Prescod, the island's first black member of the Assembly.

Opposite, take a walk through the share-taxi depot (formerly the site of the Masonic Temple) to reach **Cheapside Market**, the second big daily market in the city, first opened in 1810, which is at its finest on Saturday mornings.

Continue on down towards the sea where the Princess Alice Highway, as close as the island comes to a motorway, cuts off the fish market and fishing harbour from the main part of the town.

A couple of blocks on, you come to the **Pelican Village**, a candy-coloured low-rise shopping mall opened in 1999 with a wide array of souvenirs, arts and crafts. With a couple of excellent restaurants and cafés, it is also a great place to stop for lunch and a quick rum punch. On the far side of the road is the **Barbados Tourist Office**.

CALL ME MADAM

Rachel Pringle (1753–91) was a mulatto freedwoman who ran a somewhat notorious hotel in Bridgetown. During a wild party in 1786, the then Prince of Wales (later King William IV) comprehensively trashed the place, tipping her onto the pavement. Next day, she presented him with a bill for £700, which he paid promptly and without query, allowing her to rebuild in a grander style. The hotel was renamed the Royal Naval Hotel in the prince's honour.

BRIDGETOWN

▲ *Above: Only a handful of the old balconied houses remain in the backstreets of central Bridgetown. In the 19th century, much of the city would have looked like this.*

FIRE!

In 1845, No. 20 Swan Street was the site of one of the worst fires in the history of Barbados. The tight-packed wooden buildings created perfect conditions, and 180 houses and 4ha (10 acres) of Bridgetown were destroyed, even though the fire station was conveniently situated at the corner of James and Coleridge streets. The fire service used carts, drawn by horse or hand, with, in later years, steam pumps to help draw up water.

THE OLD CITY

Refreshed and mellow, retrace your steps back up to St Mary's Church, turn left onto Harts Street and first right onto Chapel Street. This leads through to **Swan Street**, named after a local surveyor and sea captain, John Swan, who laid out much of the street plan of the city in the 17th century. Until recently far poorer than Broad Street, although only two blocks away, and known to locals as a place to shop for textiles, Swan Street has recently had a jazzy makeover and is now a pedestrianized shopping area with patterned pavements, shady trees and benches and plenty of tourist-grabbing shops all of its own. Perhaps more importantly for tourists, Swan Street and **Roebuck Street**, around the corner and named after a notorious local tavern (a pop-ular meeting place for the early Assembly), are some of the few streets in the city to retain their 19th-century balconied houses, most of them built straight after a disastrous fire in 1840.

From Swan Street, turn left onto Henry Street, which leads through to James Street and the imposing Georgian **Barbados High Court**. The land was bought by the Barbadian government in 1682 in order to build a public warehouse. This was replaced in 1728 by an all-purpose building that housed the colony's government offices, the law courts and the jail, although the Assembly continued to meet more frequently in a more convivial atmosphere at private homes or a local tavern. The Assembly eventually moved into the Parliament Buildings in 1873 and the jail eventually closed in 1876, leaving the complex to house the law courts, magistrates' court, police station and public library (which was moved here in 1906).

Opposite the library entrance on Coleridge Street, the pretty neo-Gothic **Montefiore Fountain** was presented to the city in 1864 by John Montefiore in memory of his father. It was moved to its present location in 1940. On the corner of James and Coleridge streets, the Nicholls House is a rare surviving 17th-century relic, showing the strong Dutch influence prevalent at the time.

The Synagogue

A little further along James Street stands a well-proportioned, pale pink building. This is the **Nidhe Israel Synagogue**, built in 1654 and rebuilt after a hurricane in 1833. The first Jew was on the island by 1628, but most arrived in 1654 after they had been thrown out of Brazil by Catholic zealots and found a haven in Barbados. They rewarded the island by bringing with them the secrets of sugar refining, transforming the island's economy. Given permission to worship freely (three years ahead of London), they lost no time in building what is now the oldest synagogue in the western hemisphere. Open Monday–Friday 09:00–12:00 and 13:00–16:00, tel: 427 7611.

The number of Jews in Barbados was never huge, peaking at about 800 in the 18th century but, as elsewhere, the Jewish community, based in the Swan Street area, was highly successful and extremely influential in the commercial life of the colony. Numbers eventually dwindled until the last surviving member of the synagogue, Edmund Baeza, sold it in 1925. In 1931, Moses Altman became the first of a new group of Jewish immigrants, most fleeing from Nazi persecution, and there is now a small Jewish community back on the island.

In 1983, the community – spearheaded by Altman's grandson, Paul, and with the aid of the National Trust – bought back the synagogue and has carefully restored it to its former glory. Outside, the cemetery has graves dating from the 17th to 19th centuries, with inscriptions in English, Hebrew and even Portuguese.

Walk down the High Street, past the Parliament Buildings, to get back to National Heroes Square.

▼ *Below: Nidhe Israel Synagogue has only a tiny congregation but it also has a huge overseas following that has helped to restore and preserve the ancient building.*

3
Around Bridgetown

From its tiny central core, 'Greater' Bridgetown has sprawled out across the southwestern corner of Barbados. Over a third of the island's population lives here in chattel houses, grand Victorian mansions, Georgian shopfront apartments and modern apartment blocks. From street to street, the atmosphere lurches from Africa to little England and Charleston, USA. The immediate north of the city is dominated by the port, the south by the former British Garrison, while to the east the ring roads add swirls of dual carriageways and endless looping roundabouts, all named after Bajan heroes.

NORTHWEST OF THE CITY CENTRE

Described by Robin Williams as 'baseball on Valium', it is hard for non-aficionados to understand the thrall of cricket, a game that can last for five days and still end in a draw! Yet cricket has endured and thrived. As the British Empire grew, so did the reach of cricket and, today, it is as keenly contested in countries from Australia to India. In the West Indies, cricket is king and **Kensington Oval** is the palace. First established in a field in 1882 as the home of the Pickwick Cricket Club, the Oval has grown into the finest cricket pitch in the Americas, a name rich in cricketing history. England's first touring side played here in 1895, with Andrew Sandham scoring 325 – the first test triple century. The first combined West Indies side took to the field here against the MCC (Marylebone Cricket Club, England's premier club, based at Lord's in North London) in 1910–11. In 1930, the first West Indies test was played here (England and the West Indies drew). In 2006, the ground was

DON'T MISS

** Mount Gay Rum Factory: supposedly the world's finest rum, with tasting.
** Barbados Museum: the old British military jail.
* Garrison Savannah: parade ground turned race track.
* Kensington Oval: the cathedral of cricket.
* Tyrol Cot: crafty heritage home and political pilgrimage.

◀ *Opposite: The tourist boats all leave from Shallow Draft.*

AROUND BRIDGETOWN

shut and completely redeveloped at a cost of around US$100 million for its greatest challenge yet – hosting the final of the 2007 Cricket World Cup, with Australia beating Sri Lanka on the day. Fabulous new stands were built, taking the capacity of the ground to 32,000. Now nobody is entirely sure what to do with them. The grounds have been used for some other events, such as Cropover celebrations, but few things on the island are large enough to attract such mammoth crowds. There are guided tours every half-hour daily Mon–Fri 09:00–15:30, tel: 274 1200, web: http://kensingtonoval.org/2013/11/kensington-oval-tours/

Cruising

For an island so isolated a good harbour is essential and over the years it became necessary to move away from the tiny Careenage to the Shallow Draft and then on to the current **Deep Water Harbour**, which has been redredged and expanded still further in recent years to allow ever bigger ships, from super-tankers to cruise ships, to dock here. Open daily, University Row, Princess Alice Highway, tel: 434 6100, www.barbadosport.com

Cruising is big business here and on most days throughout the winter season, visitors will see a vast cruise ship towering over Bridgetown. Eighteen major liners use Barbados as their home port, returning here every 1–2 weeks, bringing some 500,000 visitors to the island each year. Relatively few will stay more than a day but the cruise terminal doubles as a huge shopping village with duty-free shops, designer retailers and market stalls set up in traditional chattel-house style to offer passengers a 'Barbados' experience without their ever leaving the port.

▼ *Below: Tourist boats come in all shapes and sizes, from pirate ships to speedboats.*

Around Bridgetown

In 2006, a new cruise pier was built to enable the port (in fact only around 19 percent leave the terminal area) to handle two major cruise ships simultaneously. In spite of a recent downturn in cruise traffic, a brand new larger cruise terminal, a few miles out of Bridgeport at Sugar Point, is undergoing final planning consent with a view to bringing in even more happy cruisers. Just to the north of the main port, **Shallow Draft** is the home of many of the island's pleasure craft, from the *Tiami Catamarans* to the *Atlantis* submarine (*see* pages 103 and 107).

A few blocks walk from the cruise terminal is the boutique **Agapey Chocolate Factory**, Old Colgate Palmolive Building, Harbour Industrial Park, Bridgetown, tel: 426 8505, web: www.agapey.com One tour daily at 09:30. Take a couple of hours to indulge yourself learning and tasting all about silky smooth dark chocolate, laced with island flavours from rum caramel to nutmeg.

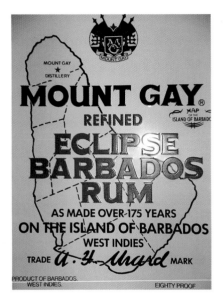

▲ Above: The Mount Gay logo has become world famous. Try the drink, the chocolates and the cake.

A short distance inland, carvers at the **Medford Craft World** specialize in beautiful wood carving, using mahogany (*see also* page 8, and panel, page 85) trees that have been officially felled or have fallen on their own, so you can buy carvings without guilt. Open daily 09:00–18:00, White Hall, Main Road, St Michael, tel: 425 1919, www.medford-craftworld.com

Yo, Ho, Ho ...

A designated driver may well be a useful addition to your party as you continue north up the main coast road to the **Mount Gay Rum Factory**. Rum was already being distilled on Barbados by 1630 and within the next 20 years, with the growth of the sugar-cane fields, it became one of the island's most successful industries. In 1655, the navy instituted a daily ration of 'grog' (rum) for all sailors, guaranteeing the industry's success. The first recorded Mount Gay rum was distilled in 1703, officially the oldest brand in the world. It is also one of the finest, frequently winning awards.

The creation of a fine rum is a blend of both art and science, as delicate as the production of a malt whisky or brandy. There are white, golden (amber-coloured) and dark rums, with different varieties produced for cooking, mixing (cocktails) and sipping (drinking neat). Dark rums are usually younger, the colour added by caramel or coffee. The crucial ingredients include sugar molasses and pure coral-filtered water in oak barrels – those used here are slightly charred old Bourbon barrels imported from Kentucky, which give the rum its rich, smoky aroma. At Mount Gay, only white and golden rums are made, with two separate distillation methods: one is the continuous method using a column still to produce a higher volume, higher alcohol content

(97%) liquor, while the other involves double distilling in a smaller Cooper Pot still to create a more intense drink with a lower alcohol content (86%). The two are aged separately for up to 25 years before blending for the final drink. The tour takes in the history of rum and the Mount Gay factory, a look at the distillery and a tasting session in the bar. The restaurant makes a good lunch stop and the shop has a wide range of rum-based souvenirs. Hourly tours Mon–Fri 09:30–15:30, plus lunch tours Tue and Thu 12:00, and cocktail tour Wed 14:00, Sat 10:30–14:30 (high season), tel: 227 8800, www. mountgayrum.com

Further up the coast, you can spend the rest of the day chilling out on **Brighton Beach**, the closest west-coast beach to Bridgetown and home of the **Cockspur Beach Club**. Open Mon–Fri 09:00–17:00, Spring Garden Highway, Brighton, Black Rock, St Michael, tel: 425 9393. The West Indies Rum Distillery is part of the complex and while tours are no longer on the menu, the flavoured rums it has pioneered from Malibu (the white rum with coconut that became a byword of Caribbean party nights) to the new Blue Chair Bay Rum which also comes in coconut, spiced and banana flavours, are freely available for imbibing on the beach. Water sports are on offer for those sober enough to indulge.

> **'...A HELLISH AND TERRIBLE LIQUOR'**
>
> Rum was already the drink of choice on the Barbados waterfront in the 1640s. Its name derives from an old English word, 'rumbullion', meaning the sort of hooligan mayhem that ensued after drinking too much rum (possibly also the derivation of *West Side Story*'s 'rumble'). In 1655, British Admiral Penn introduced a 'grog' (rum) ration for all his sailors and in 1775, during the Napoleonic Wars, rum replaced brandy as the official spirit ration of the British navy.

◄ *Left: A visitor wanders along an otherwise empty beach near Bridgetown.*

AROUND BRIDGETOWN

CRICKET LEGENDS MUSEUM

As a way of raising money to support the game and help train the next generation of players, the 42 living super-stars of Barbadian cricket have got together and formed a company, the **Cricketing Legends of Barbados**. As well as a museum filled with memorabilia, press clippings and photos, there is a website and a shop full of branded goods, and there are occa-sional events where where you can meet the great men. Herbert House Fontabelle, St Michael, tel: 227 2651, www.facebook.com/pages/Cricket-Legends-of-Barba-dos/108537345911165 Open Mon–Fri 09:00–16:30, Sat 09:00–15:00.

SEEING STARS

Built in 1963, the Harry Bayley Observatory (Highway 6, Highgate, tel: 622 2000, www.hbo.bb) is the only one in the Eastern Caribbean. Tours on Fri 20:00–22:00, weather permitting. The Friday night tour starts with a 30-minute video before you are taken up onto the roof for a turn with the 14-inch reflector telescope with which you can probe objects in deep space masked by light pollution in Europe and North America.

NORTH AND EAST OF THE CITY

Tyrol Cot Heritage Village was once the home of Sir Grantley and Lady Adams (see panel, page 21), first premier of Barbados, and the birthplace of Tom Adams, the island's second prime minister. The house, a low-rise tropical neo-Palladian villa built in 1854, has been carefully restored and is now run by the Barbados National Trust (see page 50). Inside, it is a fascinating historical snapshot, filled with antiques and political memorabilia. In the grounds several small shops and workshops, modelled on traditional chattel houses, sell a wide range of local arts and crafts. Other reconstructed buildings, which represent a cross-section of the island's traditional architecture, include a rum shop, a blacksmith's forge and a wattle-and-daub slave hut. The Stables Restaurant serves typical Bajan food (lunch only). Open Monday–Friday 09:00–17:00, Codrington Hill, St Michael, tel: 424 2074.

Close by is the **National Stadium**, opened in 1970, which seats 5000 and is used for sports meets, football, concerts and, perhaps most importantly, for judging the Crop Over costumes during the Grand Kadooment Day Parade.

From here, head out to the main ring road, the Errol Barrow Highway, turn east and follow it round. Most of the island's roundabouts are dedicated to famous Barbadians – many of them cricketers and amongst those on this road is one with a statue of the most famous cricketer of them all, Sir Garfield (Gary) Sobers (see panel, page 44). At the busy Haggatt Hall roundabout, take your life in your hands and cross over to the central island for a closer look at the magnificent **Emancipation Monument**. Also known as The Freed Slave or, more simply, 'the Bussa statue', this wonder-ful depiction of a slave breaking free of his shackles was created by Barbadian sculptor Karl Broodhagen in 1986 to commemorate the heroes of the 1816 slave uprising.

Little is known about Bussa, a slave at Bayley's Plantation in St Philip, who was possibly African-born and probably the leader of the revolution, during which he was killed. He is now a national hero, symbolizing his many nameless colleagues.

Head directly back into Bridgetown down Two Mile Hill and you pass **Government House**, the official residence of the British governor general since 1703. Named Great Pilgrim House, it was bought by the Crown in 1736 for £1350, and substantially altered in 1755. Just out of the town centre, **Queen's Park** was rented as the site of the first British garrison during the American War of Independence, while elegant **Queen's Park House** became the home of the British general commanding the garrison. After both garrison and commander left in 1906, it became a public park. In the park are a pair of giant baobab trees, thought to have been brought to the island from Guinea in 1738, the larger of the two over 18m (59ft) in circumference. Queen's Park House, once the home of the British garrison commander, is now an art gallery (tel: 427 2345, open daily 09:00–17:00, free).

▼ *Below: Karl Broodhagen's triumphant Emancipation Monument, modelled on slave rebel leader, Bussa.*

Wildey

In Wildey, a little further to the southeast, the vast and impressive **Sir Garfield Sobers Sports Complex** has a 5000-seat indoor stadium, facilities for a wide range of sports, including swimming, and an Astroturf hockey pitch; it is used not only by locals, but by visiting professional sports teams who come to the island in order to train (tel: 437 6010, www.gymnasiumltd.com.bb/html/aboutus.cfm).

Nearby, **Wildey House** is a beautiful Georgian mansion, its classic proportions adapted to withstand hurricanes, set in 2ha (5 acres) of woodland and garden. Very carefully restored and still containing furniture, china and crystal that belonged to its last owner, Edna Leacock, it is also now the

AROUND BRIDGETOWN

GARRISON LIFE

It may be a paradise island, but it was anything but for the soldiers garrisoned here in the mid-19th century. Most lived under canvas, and the few facilities available were dirty and verminous, resulting in outbreaks of disease, from cholera to yellow fever. With little to do all day, alcoholism and venereal disease were also rampant. Life gradually improved as more barracks were built and the garrison gained a proper hospital and chaplaincy, along with entertainment.

headquarters of the **Barbados National Trust** (tel: 426 2421, www.barbadosnationaltrust.org), founded in 1961, which works for the preservation of the island's historic, architectural and natural heritage, manages several of the island's historic properties as well as running open house and garden weekends and walking tours (*see* pages 101–103). Open Mon–Fri 08:30–16:30.

There is another national institution in Wildey – the **Banks Brewery**. Founded in 1961, the pilsner-style lager produced here is the other drink of choice (if rum is not your tipple) on the island and its fame has spread across the Caribbean. Sadly, at present, the factory is not running tours but tasting is possible in any island bar.

SOUTHEAST OF THE CITY CENTRE

Highlights of the city's southeast – occasionally referred to as the army district – include the Garrison (comprising the Garrison Savannah, the National Cannon Collection, St Ann's Fort, the Barbados Museum and George Washington House), as well as Aquatic Gap and Needham's Point.

▼ *Below: A 19th-century print of a formal ceremony on the Garrison parade ground, now in the Barbados Museum.*

The Garrison

About 3km (2 miles) to the south-east of the city centre is the historic army district of the island. Regiments were stationed here on and off from 1660 onwards, although it was only the outbreak of the American War of Independence that persuaded the authorities that a permanent military presence was required. Some 60-odd buildings are still standing, most of them now used for other purposes, although a few remain derelict. A detailed guide, *The Garrison and its Buildings*, is available from local book-shops. The **Garrison Savannah**, at the heart of the complex, was once the parade ground. Now it is the home of the Barbadian Turf Club, with a regular season of high-profile horse racing (*see* page 100). It was also here that the flag was raised during the independence celebrations on 30 November

▲ *Above: The Main Guard, Garrison, Bridgetown.*

1966. The west side is home to some of the **National Cannon Collection**, which includes one of only two surviving cannon stamped with Cromwell's crest (they were all struck off with the restoration of the monarchy). So far over 400, ranging in age from 1620 to 1870, have been found and catalogued on the island.

The dark red building with the clock tower (dated 1803) next door is the **Main Guard** (open Mon–Thur 07:45–16:00, Fri 07:45–14:45, tel: 426 0982), used as a guardhouse and for court martials. It now hosts temporary exhibitions and you can ask here about walking tours of the historic Garrison. Just to the south of this is the hexagonal **St Ann's Fort**, built in 1713 to bolster the island's defences against possible French invasion. It remained the property of the island militia until it was incorporated into the main garrison

WORLD CLASS

In 2011, historic Bridgetown and the Garrison were declared a UNESCO World Heritage Site, partly because of its historic importance in establishing trans-Atlantic trade and key role in developing the British colonies, partly for its status as the earliest British army and navy base in the Caribbean. The street layout of both the town and garrison remain untouched and many of the original buildings survive.

AROUND BRIDGETOWN

BAJAN DIALECT

Although basically English, the true Bajan dialect seems to be another language entirely: fruity, colourful and imaginative. Words come from several West African languages, direct translations (such as 'cry water' for tears) and archaic English. Lose the th sound, pronouns such as 'his' and 'him' and a few letters here and there; use the present tense for the past and add a healthy dose of wise sayings and proverbs, and it comes out something like, 'He does wear de new ha' when he go to church wid she' (He wore the new hat when he went to church with her). *See also* panel, page 107.

▼ *Below: The Barbados Museum, Bridgetown.*

in 1811. Today it is back in use by the Barbados Defence Force and is not open to the public.

On the far side of the Savannah, housed in the very elegant old British military jail, is the **Barbados Museum**. The museum is small, but has a fascinating and well-displayed collection, starting with the island's oldest Tainos and Carib communities, the planters and slaves, going right up to modern cricket memorabilia. Photographs and personal testimony, including slave journals, bring an immediacy to the more formal displays. The map collection includes Richard Ligon's first 1657 map of the island, while a Children's Gallery helps explain history to younger minds. It is open Monday–Saturday 09:00–17:00, Sunday 14:00–18:00, Highway 7, Garrison Savannah, tel: 427 0201, website: www.barbmuse.org.bb

In 1751, George Washington, aged 19, stayed in Barbados for about 10 weeks – the only trip he ever made outside the USA. They were trying to find a cure for Lawrence Washington's TB, but George promptly caught smallpox. Both brothers survived. Although his stay was short, the restored Bush Hill House was renamed **George Washington House**, and the plaque commemorating the visit was unveiled by Bill Clinton in 1997. The house is now decorated roughly as it would have been when George visited, with displays not only of furniture but of the medical equipment used to treat smallpox, and the slavegoods which he, as a slave owner, would have used. It is open Monday–Friday 09:00–16:30, Bush Hill, tel: 228 5461, www.georgewashington barbados.org

Aquatic Gap and Needham's Point

Carlisle Bay, the broad sweep of sand between Bridgetown and Needham's Point, neatly marks the transition from historic Bridgetown to the touristy south coast.

With the Hilton Hotel (*see* page 113) firmly in residence on the point, it has a fine – if overcrowded – beach, backed by an esplanade with a fabulous view of the sunset, and is also home to two of the island's wildest party playgrounds – Harbour Lights and The Boatyard (*see* page 118), both of which offer day and night drinking, dancing and music. However, this is also still part of the old Garrison district and there is plenty on offer for history buffs, both on land and in the water.

▲ *Above: The Harbour Lights club offers everything, from calypso to disco.*

On the waterfront beside the hotel, **Fort Charles** is the oldest of the forts on the island, built as wooden Needham's Fort in 1650, only 23 years after the settlement, to protect the royalist island against attack by Oliver Cromwell's Commonwealth army. The restoration of the monarchy in 1660 was marked by a prompt change of name to Fort Charles, after the new king. It was redesigned and more heavily fortified in 1705, but remained part of the Barbados militia until 1836. Behind the hotel is the British military cemetery.

Off-shore, the bay offers some of the best **diving** on the island (*see* panel, page 95), thanks to seven wrecks sunk over the years that are not only fascinating historically but have become artificial reefs, attracting an array of fish and corals.

4
The South Coast

If the west coast is the place to be seen, the south coast is quite definitely the place to be heard. This is the island's party playground, with rows of mass-market hotels, apartments and timeshare resorts, clubs, pubs and restaurants lined up along Highway 7 in a seamless ribbon of towns that sound more like England than the Caribbean – Hastings, Worthing, Dover and Scarborough. Generally speaking (but with some notable exceptions), this is the younger, less sophisticated, more child-friendly and cheaper part of the island. Shaped like an open V, the south coast slopes gently down to South Point, its beaches as broad and white, its seas as gentle as those on the west coast. Beyond this, heading northeast past the airport towards the east coast, are the rockier bays and wilder waters of the Atlantic seaboard. Highway 7 shadows the coastline for much of the way.

HASTINGS TO WORTHING

Just beyond the Garrison area (*see* page 51), Hastings has no beach, but does have a lovely seafront esplanade, ideal for strolling and watching the sunset. The red-brick Pavilion Court apartments were once the barracks for St Ann's Fort. Within the complex, a local enthusiast has opened his collection of vintage motors to the public. The **Mallalieu Motor Collection** contains some magnificent cars, from a 1947 Bentley to a 1965 Vanden Plas Princess once used by the governor general. Show any interest and you will get a personal tour by the owner and may even get a drive in the

DON'T MISS

*** **The Beaches:** some of the finest sand on the island.
*** **Oistins Fish Fry:** where Barbados goes to party.
*** **St Lawrence Gap:** where the tourists go to party.
*** **Concorde Experience:** your chance to fantasize aboard the world's most glamorous passenger plane.

◄ *Opposite: Frying in the sun on Dover Beach.*

car of your choice. The Mallalieu Motor Collection is open Sat–Sun 08:00–17:00 by appointment (Pavilion Court, Hastings Road, tel: 426 4640, www.fiaheritagemuseums.com/47-mallalieu-motor-collection.html).

Just to the north of town is the **Wanderers' Cricket Club** (Dayrells Road, Christ Church, tel: 427 7415, www.facebook.com/WanderersBarbados/timeline), home to the island's oldest cricket club, founded in 1877. It still has an active programme of matches and hosts festivals, including the International Masters Football Festival (last week of May). In October 2006, the third Vintage Cricket Festival brought in teams from across the world.

The next town along is **Rockley**, home to one of the island's most famous beaches. **Accra Beach** is perpetually crowded, with beach games, lifeguards, bars and wandering vendors that provide a real party atmosphere. There is shade under the casuarina trees and a wide range of water sports, from windsurfing to body surfing, with just enough waves to make it exciting. Across the road, the **Quayside Centre** offers a little alternative retail therapy. A short distance inland, the nine-hole **Rockley Golf Club** (tel: 435 7873, website: www.rockleygolfclub.com)

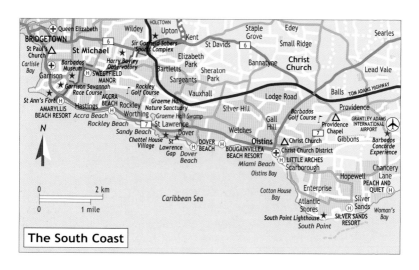

The South Coast

meanders through a residential development, and welcomes all ages and levels of competence. Non-members pay more, but Fridays offer a two-for-one deal on green fees.

There are fewer people, but still plenty of life, on **Sandy Beach** in **Worthing**, the next town along the chain, its waters calmed by an offshore reef that is one of several excellent dive sites dotted along the south coast.

The Last Mangrove

With the heavy development – both by earlier planters and the modern tourist trade – the mangroves that once protected the island's shores have all but disappeared. The only surviving remnant was the 32ha (79-acre) Graeme Hall Swamp and Nature Sanctuary. Unlike anything else in Barbados, this wonderful wilderness park was based around a swamp and a lagoon, its boardwalk offering viewing points through tangled red-and-white mangroves to where snowy white little egrets and charcoal-blue herons stand still as statues in the sedges. Flashing fluorescent hummingbirds flit through the branches and sandpipers and coots paddle in the shallows. Around 150 species of migrant birds stop here for a breather, with up to 20 of the 40 species on the island choosing to nest in the sanctuary each year. In the water, there are some 40 species of fish, while huge cane toads – reaching a size of up to 22cm (8.5in) long – and tiny tree frogs croak and whistle the backing track. Sadly most of this idyllic reserve remains closed (only the coffee shop and main lawn are currently open to the public) as it battles to achieve protected status from the developers for one of the island's last and richest havens of wildlife. To see more on the debate and to add your voice, visit www.graeme hall.com

MANGROVES

There are many species of mangrove, growing in brackish coastal swamps in tropical and subtropical regions throughout the world. They perform many vital services in the local ecology, their tangled roots helping to knit together fragile earth and rock, offering protection from tidal erosion. They are also valuable nurseries for fish, amphibians, land animals and birds. In spite of this, however, over 50% of the world's mangroves have already been lost. The only mangroves remaining on Barbados are in the now closed Graeme Hall Nature Sanctuary.

▼ Below: The mangrove lagoons are a breeding ground for birds, fish and amphibians.

THE SOUTH COAST

RUM PUNCH

- One of sour (lime juice)
- Two of sweet (cane syrup)
- Three of strong (Barbados rum)
- Four of weak (water or fruit juice)
- Five dashes of angostura bitters (optional)
- Nutmeg (optional)
- Serve in a tall glass on the rocks.

Invented by Admiral Vernon, 1731.

Dancing the Night Away

St Lawrence Gap is the social centre of the south coast, crammed with hotels, bars, restaurants and clubs. It really does have something for everyone, from huge establishments such as the super-smooth Sugar Ultra Lounge or the Reggae Lounge (see page 118) and more elegant fine-dining options such as Josef's (see page 117) to laid-back live music in venues such as the Old Jamm Inn (see page 118). Nearby, the **Chattel House Village** is a thoroughly modern craft centre in a series of reproduction chattel houses, while **Dover Beach**, lined by hotels, offers fine white sand, beach bars and water sports. This is the home of **Da Congaline Carnival** for four days in late April every year, one of the wildest celebrations of music, dance and food on an island that loves to celebrate.

Beyond Dover, **Oistins** – at one end of magnificent **Miami Beach** (a.k.a. Enterprise Beach) – is the island's main fishing village and was the spot where, in 1639, Cromwell's troops finally managed to land and quell the rebellious, royalist island. But none of these are what have made it one of the most popular attractions on Barbados. For much of the week, it is a quiet village, made busy for a few hours a day when the fishing fleet comes in. But on Friday evening all that changes. The rum shops throw open their doors, the fish market and the surrounding streets are transformed into a vast open-air barbecue, lights and sound stages are plugged in and the bands strike up – reggae at one end of the market, old-time ballroom at the other and a gloriously clashing cacophony of

▼ *Below: Getting to know you – locals and tourists bond over volleyball on Worthing beach.*

sound if you stand at the wrong spot halfway between. Literally thousands of people, locals and tourists alike, pour into town to queue for freshly fried marlin and chips on paper plates, washed down by Banks beer straight from the bottle and topped off by several tots of sippin' rum. Stay with the crush or take your plate down to the beach to watch the moonlight dance on the water. The party goes on until the wee small hours. If you can't make it on a Friday night, there are lesser versions on Thursday and Saturday, and Easter takes on a distinctly fishy feel with the annual **Oistins Festival**.

▲ Above: Fish and chips under the stars at the Oistins Friday night fish fry – where the food and drinks are cheap, the company and the music cool.

Queen of the Skies

Inland, the **Barbados Golf Club** (Durants, tel: 428 8463, www.barbadosgolfclub.com) is the only totally public 18-hole golf course. Nearby, the Grantley Adams Airport (*see* page 121) sprawls along the coast. And did you ever wonder what happened to Concorde when she retired? Wonder no more. One of the gloriously sleek super-planes has made its home at the **Barbados Concorde Experience**, Grantley Adams International Airport, Christ Church, tel: 246 420 7738, www.barbadosconcorde.com (open daily 09:00–18:00). Developed as an Anglo-French project, Concorde first flew in 1969, entering service in 1976, with the last flight on 26 November 2003. Only 20 planes were ever built. Although several have been lovingly restored, experts agree that it is now impossible for them ever to fly again. She flew at an average cruising speed of 2140kph (1334mph), about twice the speed of any other passenger aircraft, and is still the only supersonic passenger aircraft to enter service.

5
The West Coast

Of course, it may all depend on your tastes and your pocket, but if you are searching for a Caribbean paradise, the Platinum Coast is the place to stay. This is the reef-protected side of Barbados, low-lying and shallow sloping, where holiday brochure clichés come to life on golden beaches. The beautiful people lie on sunbeds, gently baking while smiling waiters ply them with an endless supply of rum punch decorated with fruit and small umbrellas. Every so often, they will stand, stretch and wander off to play golf or have a massage. Offshore, local lads roar along the coast, spray and dreadlocks flying, looking for customers for jetski rides and a fine night's loving – both in good supply. As the sun sets over the sea and the frog chorus tunes up, the candles are lit at terrace tables all along the bay and the finest gourmet restaurants throw open their doors.

Keep your eyes open – there are paparazzi permanently in the area looking for celebrities to snap and there are plenty around in season, although the real A-listers tend to hide behind high walls and heavy security in lavish private mansions. Property prices are at record highs here, with the owners of the last few chattel houses with beach access being offered millions of dollars for their land. They will probably not hold out much longer, although as one man has been quoted as saying, 'Why do I need their millions of dollars, when all I would want to do with it is buy myself a beachfront property – and I already have that.' He has a point. If you don't have a beachfront house or even hotel, there are plenty

Don't Miss

*** **The Beaches:** fine sand, turquoise seas, palm trees and the setting sun.
*** **Turtles:** nesting beaches, people-friendly swimmers.
*** **Restaurants and hotels:** join all the beautiful people in paradise.
** **Golf:** world-class courses.
* **Holetown:** the island's first official settlement.

◄ *Opposite: White sand, coconut palms, turquoise seas and coral reefs – the Platinum Coast is the perfect tropical beach.*

THE WEST COAST

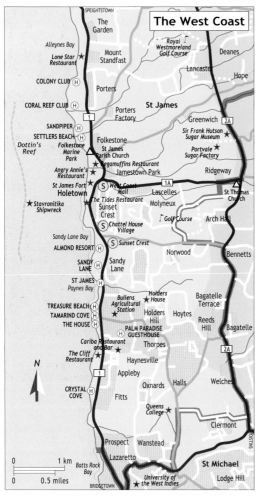

The West Coast

of paths that will allow you to thread your way down between the hotel grounds onto the beaches, which are all public.

Turning Turtle

Heading north along the coast from Bridgetown, **Batts Rock Bay** and **Prospect Beach** are both used mainly by locals. A little further along, **Paynes Bay** is one of the finest on the island, home to several hotels including the enchanting little Treasure Beach and The House. This is also where the turtles hang out and every morning, from around 11:00 onwards, boats crowd in to the area and boatmen feed the **turtles** to attract them in. If you don't fancy the organized tour (*see page 108*), they are generally close enough for reasonable swimmers to join them from the beach — although it would be wise to keep a lookout for boats that can run you down in the scrimmage. Swimming back to shore is harder than going out, even with flippers, so save some energy for fighting the currents.

The Good Life

Just inland from Paynes Bay, **Holders House** is a glorious

17th-century plantation home set in 4ha (10 acres) of manicured gardens. It is privately owned and the house is normally closed to the public, although you may get in on one of the National Trust Open House days (*see* page 102). You can visit the gardens during the weekly Sunday Farmers' Market (09:00–14:00, www.holders-farmersmarket.com). However, it is also home to the island's main arts festival. For two weeks in March, the **Holders Season** (tel: 432 6385, http://holdersseason.com) brings in top names in theatre and music (from jazz to classical) for magical performances in the open-air theatre. Barbados Polo Club (*see* page 105) is just above the house on Holders Hill.

▲ *Above: The swimming pool at Sandy Lane is like the set of a movie.*

Continuing north, **Sandy Lane** (www.sandylane.com) is without doubt the most famous and expensive hotel on the island (its private villa is a mere US$25,000 a night). As well as a fabulous beachfront, a **spa** (tel: 444 2100) and pool straight out of a Hollywood fantasy, the hotel runs the island's top **golf club** (tel: 444 2500), with two 18-hole championship courses (the Country Club course and Tom Fazio-designed Green Monkey course) as well as the Old Nine (nine-hole course). Tiger Woods chose Sandy Lane as the venue for his now infamous wedding to Swedish girlfriend, Elin Nordegren, here in 2004, hiring the whole hotel for his guests, who included Michael Jordan, Oprah Winfrey and Bill Gates. In 2006, the golf course hosted the World Golf Championship. The club is open to non-hotel residents, and there are also a number of villas for rent or sale along the courses.

THE WEST COAST

▲ *Above: Post office and police station, the old St James Fort in Holetown is still the official centre of the town.*

HOLETOWN

On 17 February 1627, the *William and John* arrived in Barbados carrying the colony's first settlers, 80 English men, women and children, and 10 African slaves they had picked up en route. They landed and built their first town at Jamestown (named after King James II, who – unknown to them – had actually died while they were at sea, and later renamed Holetown after a tidal hole near the beach). Today, the old **St James Fort** is now the police station and post office, only a few leftover cannons in the grounds marking its previous role. The monument here marks both the first English landing, led by Captain John Powell, in July 1625 and the 1627 landing, led by his brother, Henry. The monument dates to 1905 when the locals mistakenly celebrated their 300th anniversary 20 years too soon. Each February, the town celebrates the anniversary of the 1627 landing with the week-long **Holetown Festival**, one of the most vibrant on the island, with parades, music, dance, and a street fair with crafts, food and drink stalls.

These days, Holetown is very much a tourist centre with a wide range of excellent cafés and restaurants, a great beach bar and public beach, numerous small boutiques and three shopping malls: **Sunset Crest**, the **Chattel House Village** and the **West Coast Mall**.

St James

There is a pretty Methodist church in the town centre but **St James Parish Church** (open daily 08:00–18:00, tel: 422 4117) is located in the north of the town. The first wooden church was built here in 1628, and replaced in coral stone in 1660. The church was enlarged in 1874 and a stained-glass window of the Ascension added as a war memorial in 1924. The church contains the graves of many of the early settlers, along with extracts of early records – although the archives themselves have been moved to the Barbados Museum. The font (1684) and bell (1696), inscribed with 'God Bless King William', are among the old-est in the Americas. The church also contains a mural of Sir John Gay Alleyne (1724–1801), speaker of the Barbadian Parliament, whose former home, **Porters Great House**, is 1km (½ mile) further north. The only way to see the house is to rent it out as a holiday let – for healthily vast amounts of money.

Back on the beach, **Folkestone Marine Park** is the centre of a marine reserve that stretches along the coast for some 2.2km (1½ miles) and reaches 950m (3000ft) out to sea, protecting some of the island's finest coral reefs and the *Stavronikita* wreck dive site. There is a small eco-museum and a basic shop, but the real joys here are the picnic facilities popular with locals at weekends and the offshore action with snorkels and scuba gear for hire, changing facilities and lockers. Glass-bottomed boats will take non-swimmers out to the reef. It is open daily 09:00–17:00, Church Point, Holetown, tel: 422 2314.

Inland, beside Highway 2a, the **Portvale Sugar Factory** is one of two remaining on the island, a massive industrial complex that takes in raw cane straight from the fields, turning out the granulated sugar and molasses that go to make rum. In the grounds, the **Sir Frank Hutson Sugar Museum**, now run by the National Trust, is a fascinating collection of the machinery used in sugar production, displayed alongside old photos. Take time to talk to the curator who knows everything there is to know on the subject. In the sugar season (February–May), he will also happily take you on a guided tour of the modern factory. It is open Monday–Saturday 09:00–17:00, tel: 432 0100.

From here, the road continues northward – past the **Royal Westmoreland Golf Course**, one of the finest courses in the Caribbean but only open to members – to Speightstown (*see* page 81).

> **WELL-HATCHED BY MOONLIGHT**
>
> Most of the beaches along the west coast are turtle-breeding beaches and there are strict controls to ensure the safety of the eggs. In hatching season, lights in the hotels are dimmed as they can confuse the hatchlings, which use the moonlight on the water to guide their first scramble from the nest to the relative safety of the ocean. Guests are allowed to watch both nesting and hatching under strict supervision and may be recruited to scoop up strays and put them back on the path to the sea.

▼ *Below: To market, to market – local goods are available everywhere.*

6
The East Coast

Heading east past Grantley Adams International Airport, the nature of the coast soon begins to change as the ground tilts upwards, creating high cliffs, and the gentle Caribbean gives way to the furious force of the Atlantic weather. Here most of the coast is cliffy, while beaches are mostly small coves reached by steep tracks and stairs, vicious currents swirl through the surrounding rocks and high winds perpetually batter the ears.

Crane Beach (named after a massive crane that once stood in the local harbour) is celebrated by many, for no apparent reason, as one of the finest in the Caribbean. The beach is attractive, but it is overlooked and overused by the growing timeshare resort above. And while it is nominally public, the resort charges non-residents steeply to use their 88-step staircase down the cliff. There are plans to build a lift.

Sam Lord's Castle

About 3km (2 miles) northeast of The Crane, overlooking Long Bay, **Sam Lord's Castle** — one of the more famous houses on the island — was built in the 1820s by Sam Lord, who died owing a fortune, although he is said to have made one by luring ships onto the rocks then stripping the wrecks for salvage. It was an ostentatiously opulent house that ran for a while as a hotel, before being left to become derelict and eventually, in 2010, to burn in somewhat dubious circumstances. In late 2014, it was announced that the site had been compulsorily purchased by the Barbadian Government and a new 450-room hotel, funded by the Chinese was about to rise, like a phoenix,

---

DON'T MISS

*** **Andromeda Botanic Gardens:** a truly lush tropical botanical masterpiece.
*** **The Views:** of the wild and rocky Atlantic coast.
** **Bathsheba:** the only town on the east coast.
* **Crane Beach:** claimed to be one of the finest beaches in the world.
* **St John's Church:** Anglican tradition on the cliffs.

◀ *Opposite: Atlantic waves have carved rock sculptures off the beach at Bathsheba.*

▲ *Above: Codrington College offers an elegant start to a career in the cloth.*

from the ashes.

Just north of here is a trio of delightful white sand beaches where you will often find yourself in splendid isolation: **Cave Bay**, **Harrismith Bay**, reached through the grounds of the semi-derelict Harrismith Great House, and **Bottom Bay**. The area looks less than its shining best at present as work began on a major new resort complex to include 101 villas, 600 apartments, a hotel and spa, only for it to be abandoned, amidst possible accusations of fraud. It will be years before it's all sorted out.

From here, the island reaches its easternmost tip at **Ragged Point**, marked by the **East Point Lighthouse** (which is not open to the public), from where there are spectacular views right the way along the east coast.

OCEAN VIEWS

From here, roads along the top of the island's escarpment offer one fabulous coastal view after another. One of the finest is from the grounds of **Codrington College** (www.codrington.org), above Conset Bay. Founded in 1743, with money left by Christopher Codrington III, a Barbadian who became governor of the Leeward Islands, to the Society for the Propagation of the Gospel in Foreign Parts, it is the oldest Anglican theological college in the Americas, and is still a working seminary. Christopher actually died in 1710 but his family contested the will with vigour and it was many years before the church finally had its money. Visitors are

RED FLAG

The wild Atlantic waters of the east coast are extremely different to the gentle west. The waves may be ideal for surfers but there are complex swirling webs of currents and undertows that make it extremely dangerous to swim out of your depth. Most locals find bowls in the shallow surf and sit in them to cool down. Do the same.

welcome to wander the grounds, with their formal avenue of cabbage palm trees, lily lake and gentle nature trail.

Continuing north, you will find **St John's Church**, built in 1836 to replace the 1660 building, which was demolished in the 1831 hurricane. From the outside, it is an archetypical neo-Gothic English country church; inside it is lush with decorative wood. The pulpit, the only item salvaged from the hurricane, is made from six different woods – ebony, locust, mahogany and manchineel from Barbados, and imported oak and pine. The walls and grounds are rich in monuments, including the one of Ferdinando Paleologus, last known descendant of the brother of Constantine XI (the last Byzantine emperor). From the grounds there are, inevitably, fine views. Open daily 06:00–18:00, tel: 430 7506.

A Paradise Garden

From here, small lanes lead along the high ground past the 300m (985ft) **Hackleton's Cliff**, with great views.

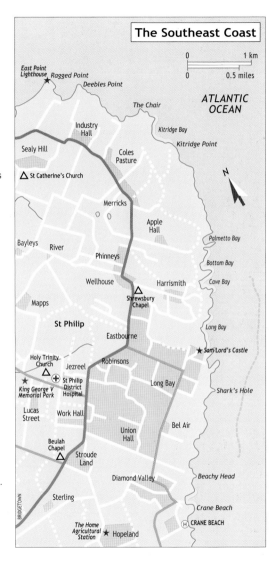

The Southeast Coast

0   1 km

0   0.5 miles

East Point Lighthouse   Ragged Point

Deebles Point

The Chair

ATLANTIC OCEAN

Industry Hall

Kitridge Bay

Kitridge Point

Sealy Hill

Coles Pasture

St Catherine's Church

Merricks

Apple Hall

Palmetto Bay

Bayleys   River

Phinneys

Bottom Bay

Wellhouse

Harrismith

Cave Bay

Mapps

Shrewsbury Chapel

St Philip

Long Bay

Eastbourne

Holy Trinity Church

Jezreel

Robinsons

King George V Memorial Park

St Philip District Hospital

Long Bay

Sam Lord's Castle

Shark's Hole

Lucas Street

Work Hall

Union Hall

Bel Air

Beulah Chapel

Stroude Land

Diamond Valley

Beachy Head

BRIDGETOWN

Sterling

Crane Beach

The Home Agricultural Station   Hopeland

CRANE BEACH

THE EAST COAST

The main road threads down through the banana plantations towards Bathsheba. En route, you will come to the 2ha (5-acre) **Andromeda Botanic Gardens**. Designed by renowned horticulturalist Iris Bannochie in 1954, and named after a Greek maiden chained to the cliff as a sacrifice to the sea monster, this is a magnificently lush tropical paradise, its steeply winding paths overhung by orchids and begonias, spiky palms, lacy ferns and the bearded figs that gave the island its name, the air filled with the breathy wings of humming-birds and butterflies, lizards scampering across hot rocks beneath. There is a also café and plenty of places to rest, breathe in the flower-rich air, and admire the beautiful gardens – as well as the view. Open daily 09:00–17:00, tel: 433 9384, www.andromedabarbados.com

▲ Above: The lily ponds in the Andromeda Botanic Gardens, the closest thing you can get to Eden.

BATHSHEBA

The main town on the east coast of Barbados, surfside Bathsheba is probably the prettiest town on the island. There are a couple of small hotels, but few people stay here other than surfers, who hire one of the little cottages and eat in the rum shops and beach bars. There are three main surf breaks: the famed Soup Bowl (*see* panel, page 110), High Rock and Parlors, with waves reaching approximately 5–7m (16–23ft) in season (November–February).

North of here, the coast runs through increasingly remote and wild countryside, past the violent seas of the **Cattlewash**, **Barclays Park**, a popular weekend picnic spot, past **Chalky Mount** – where a group of potters produce and sell artisan earthenware – to **Belleplaine**, northern terminus of the long-defunct Barbados Railway (*see* panel, page 71).

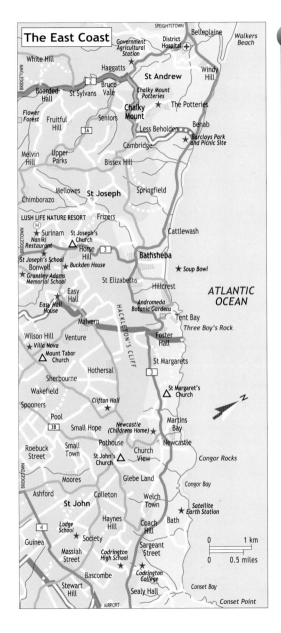

Opened in 1883, the Barbados Railway ran from Bridgetown up the east coast to Belleplaine. Built initially at 3ft 6in guage, it was narrowed to 0.76m (2ft 6in) in 1898, and coal gave way to oil during World War I. Used primarily for transporting sugar, it also proved to be a popular weekend excursion for a while, but the railway was never financially successful and cars finally drove it out of business in 1937. Little trace now remains of the line.

7
Central Barbados

Head just 2km [1¼ miles] inland and the feel of Barbados changes dramatically. Tourism all but vanishes, leaving a land of rolling green hills, with villages of chattel houses, the rustle of cane leaves in soft breezes, the low-voiced chat of the men on the veranda of a rum shop and in the distance, always, the soft blue of the sea.

ST PHILIP

In the southern parish of St Philip, two distinctly different island staples still live together. Unlikely as it may seem, Barbados has been an oil-producing nation since the 1870s, now producing around 1000 barrels a day, along with small quantities of natural gas in the **Woodbourne Oil Fields**. The oil is refined in Trinidad before being returned to the island for use, supplying about 10% of the island's needs and keeping it self-sufficient in natural gas.

There may be no oil distillery but the islanders are experts in distilling rum. The **Foursquare Rum Factory and Heritage Park** has been operating since the 1800s on an old molasses and sugar plantation, although the plant today is ultramodern. As well as a description of how to make rum and a tasting, the tour includes small museums devoted to sugar and Bajan folk culture, a tour of the bottling plant, and a glass fusing studio. If the government's plans to start producing ethanol from sugar cane come to fruition, these unlikely bedfellows will be drawn even closer.
Open Mon–Fri 09:00–17:00, Sat 10:00–21:00, Sun 12:00–18:00; tel: 420 1977.

DON'T MISS

*** Sunbury Plantation House:** ease and luxury built on slave labour.
*** Harrison's Cave:** fantasy caves and underground rivers.
** Orchid World:** an explosion of tropical colour.
** Flower Forest:** deep, steep and shady gardens.
** Earthworks Pottery:** jazzy and practical souvenirs that are dishwasher safe.

◄ *Opposite: Cutting through the cane fields – a very gentle cycle ride.*

Sunbury

Meanwhile, just up the road, **Sunbury Plantation House** is the finest of the great houses open to the public. It was first built in 1660 by Matthew Chapman, an Anglo-Irish planter and cousin of the Earl of Carlisle. The walls, 76cm (30in) thick, were made from flint and other stone brought over from England as ballast, while sturdy jalousie shutters helped protect the windows against hurricanes. It gained its name in the 1780s when it was bought by John and George Barrow who renamed it after their family home in Kent, England, rebuilding large portions of the house after disastrous hurricanes. The family was an influential one. John Henry Barrow was a horticultural pioneer, bringing in the first teak tree, as well as introducing mahogany to the island. Over 100 of his original 300 mahogany trees remain standing today. His son, John Barrow, was the colonel responsible for putting down the 1816 slave rebellion before he and his family emigrated to Newfoundland in 1835, shortly after emancipation.

The house burned down in 1995, but was carefully restored by its owners, Mr and Mrs Keith Melville, with furniture for the displays added from various other great houses around the island. The house itself is decorated as it would have been in its heyday – from the planter's chair and working desk to the nursery with its army of dolls and a bath overlooked by Queen Victoria (definitely not amused). There are also plenty of photos of life on the plantation and several collections – of kitchen utensils, horse-drawn carriages and even optical equipment (used by Mr Melville's grandfather, Dr Harcourt Carter, the island's first optician). Open daily 09:00–17:00, with the last tour at 16:30, tel: 423 6270, www.barbadosgreathouse.com

▼ *Below: Dolls wait patiently in a nursery long since turned into a museum at Sunbury Plantation House.*

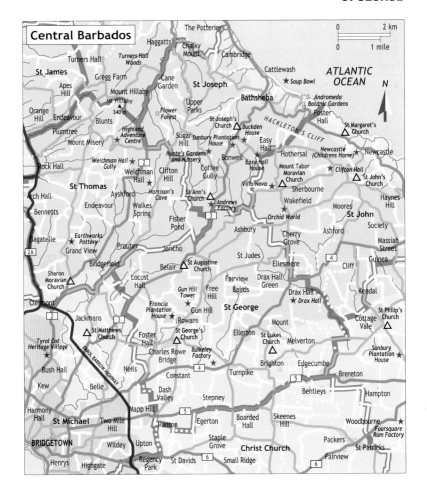

Central Barbados

ST GEORGE

St George's Valley is the real heart of sugar-production territory. In all, the island has around 1500 small farms, producing around 60,000 tons of sugar a year. Most farms are small these days, averaging only 80ha (200 acres) each, making it difficult for the owners to earn a decent living. There is an added emphasis on homegrown food

Every part of the sugar cane is used. Its matted roots help bind the island's shallow topsoil and prevent erosion. When ripe, the cane is crushed for juice, which is turned into sugar, with the remaining molasses used for rum. The sludge and cane fibre left at the end of the process are used for animal feed and ploughed back into the ground as fertilizer.

production, with many turning to growing vegetables instead. The days of the plantations are generally long gone but some do remain, usually propped up by imported money. A few kilometres northwest of Sunbury lies **Drax Hall**, built in the 1650s by William and James Drax. It is one of only three surviving Jacobean properties in the western hemisphere (*see also* page 85) and is classical in its design, with its steep gable roofs and casement gable windows. Drax Hall is not open to the public.

Due west from here, on Highway 4, **Gun Hill** is one of four points on the island where watchers kept an eye out for invasion fleets as early as 1697. The current station tower is, however, just one of half a dozen erected in 1818 after the slave rebellion of 1816 when planters suddenly realized that while the threat of French invasion had been strong, the real threat came from their own cane fields as disgruntled slaves scented freedom in the 1807 act that abolished the slave trade. The tower was used as a field hospital during outbreaks of disease such as yellow fever or cholera, and even under normal circumstances, recuperating soldiers were sent up here as watchers. One of them, Captain Henry Wilkinson, created the white lion on the slope below during his off-duty hours in 1868. There is a small display inside and the views, needless to say, are fabulous. Open Mon–Sat 09:00–17:00, tel: 429 1358, http://barbadosnationaltrust.org

▼ *Below: Order yourself a dinner service from Earthworks and have an exuberant, colourful souvenir of Barbados.*

WESTERN REGION

Nearby **Francia Plantation House**, built by a Brazilian planter in 1913, is no longer open to the public, but you can visit **St George's Church**, rebuilt in 1784 after hurricane damage, and the **Sharon Moravian Church**, rebuilt in 1833 to the exact plan of the original 1799 church. German Moravian missionaries had arrived on the island in 1765 to convert and educate the slaves. Unlike the earlier Quakers, the planters allowed them access to the church, but even so, it was over 30 years before they began to see any significant success. Today, they are one of the more influential Christian churches on the island, tel: 425 4011.

Tucked into the hillside with lovely views back down to Bridgetown, **Earthworks Pottery** began life in 1983 with a single potter, Goldie Spieler. Now run by her son David, it employs 24 people and its jazzy designs sell not only from its own shop, but from the web and in shops throughout the Caribbean. Unusually, everything is fired to stoneware temperatures and the tableware is tough enough for everyday use, and for both the microwave and dishwasher. Mix and match your own set or ask for custom designs to your own specification. As well as the pottery studio and Treehouse Café, the grounds are shared by the On the Wall Art Gallery and the Batik Studio, making this one of the best places on the island to buy high-quality souvenirs. The studio is open Monday–Friday 09:00–17:00, Saturday 09:00–13:00, 2 Edgehill Heights, St Thomas, tel: 425 0223, www.earthworks-pottery.com

▲ *Above: Orchid World is a kaleidoscope of colours so rich that some seem unreal.*

EASTERN DISTRICT

Back across towards the east coast, **Orchid World** is the second of three fabulous botanic gardens on the island (*see also* Andromeda on page 69 and the Flower Forest on page 79). This 2.4ha (6-acre) garden, a former pig and chicken farm, is now a glorious riot of colour designed to test the senses and drive photographers into raptures. Paths lead downhill through lush green formal gardens, with orchids – from the timid to the flamboyant – tucked into flowerbeds and in the crooks of tree branches. At the bottom a series of orchid houses cater to the more fragile species. There are some 20,000 orchids in the gardens, so allow plenty of time to admire them all. Open daily 09:00–17:00, Groves, tel: 433 0774, www.orchidworldbarbados.com

Nearby **Villa Nova** was once one of the great sugar plantation homes, built by Edmund Haynes after an earlier house was destroyed in the 1831 hurricane. It was owned for a while by British prime minister, Sir Anthony Eden. Restored at vast expense as a luxury hotel in the 1990s, it is yet another inland property that did not survive and now stands empty on sale at the time of writing for a mere US$9.5 million. The **Mount Tabor Moravian Church** nearby was paid for by Edmund Haynes, a staunch supporter of the missionaries.

CENTRAL BARBADOS

▲ *Above: Underground rivers have carved a magical world through the coral rock in Harrison's Cave.*

FORBIDDEN FRUIT

This miracle fruit, beloved of dieters around the world, is a Barbadian baby, first grown in Welchman Hall Gully in the 18th century, a natural cross-pollination between shaddock and sweet orange, both imported from Asia. First named the 'forbidden fruit', it was later renamed 'grapefruit' as it grows in bunches, like grapes.

SCOTLAND DISTRICT

As the land rises to **Mount Hillaby** – at 340m (1115ft), the highest point on the island – the area right at the centre of Barbados is known as the Scotland District, as it supposedly looks like the Scottish Highlands (it doesn't). It is, however, very beautiful, both above and below ground.

Virtually undetectable from the surface, **Harrison's Cave** is one of the island's most popular tourist attractions. Thought to have been used as a refuge by runaway slaves, it was opened up after exploration by Danish caver Ole Sørensen in 1970. One of a whole warren of caves carved by water percolating through the soft coral limestone, it has a magnificent array of caves and corridors, stalactites, stalagmites, rivers, pools and a 12m (40ft) waterfall. After a short introductory video, visitors tour a 1.5km (1-mile) stretch of the caves on a guided electric train, with a couple of photo stops. Expect to get damp, with water still pouring through from the surface, and numbers are limited, so get there early to ensure a place without a long queue. A recent redevelopment has added a new visitors' centre on arrival and walking trails in the surrounding valley. Open daily 08:45–15:45; Welchman Hall, Highway 2, St Thomas, tel: 417 3700.

If less commercialized caving is more to your liking, head for **Jack-in-the-Box Gully**, another part of the same giant system, where you can head into Coles Cave on your own with a hard hat and torch, or swing through the air on a bosun's chair (*see panel page 101*).

Also part of the same cave system, **Welchman Hall Gully** is now a deep open ravine with some giant stalactites and stalagmites still standing, and offers one of the finest walks on the island. Named after Asygell Williams, a royalist Welsh general who was banished here after the English Civil War, it is now maintained by the National Trust. Steep steps lead down to a 1.2km [¾-mile] path that threads past bamboo, jungle creepers, bearded fig and Judas trees, palms and ferns, mahogany and mango, opening out to spectacular views down to the coast.

Look out for cane toads, green monkeys and forest birds as well as imported trees: nutmeg and clove from the Moluccas, rubber from Malaysia and breadfruit imported by Captain Bligh of *Mutiny on the Bounty* infamy. Open daily 09:00–1700, Highway 2 (directly east of Holetown), St Thomas, tel: 438 6671, www.welchmanhallgullybarbados.com

Just to the north of Welchman Hall, the **Highland Adventure Centre** offers horseback rides through the cane fields for all levels of experience (although the minimum age is restricted to 12), as well as mountain biking and guided hikes. Open daily, 09:00–17:00, tel: 438 8069.

Also close to Welchman's Gully is the newest of the island's many magnificent gardens, **Hunte's Gardens and Nursery**. It's one man's passion – and Anthony Hunte may well be on hand to enthuse you as you walk through the steep winding paths dripping with tropical splendour while Maria Callas adds even more steamy sultriness. The garden, set around the stables of a former sugar plantation, is not huge, at 1.75 acres (just under 1 ha) but this is a garden of romance, of stirring and stillness, a place of extraordinary emotion. Castle Grant, St Joseph, tel: 433 3333, www.huntesgardensbarbados.com Open daily.

Forest of Flowers

The last of the great Bajan gardens, the 20ha (50-acre) **Flower Forest** is again steeply wooded, with a 1km (2/3-mile) path threading down the lavishly landscaped hillside, site of a derelict sugar plantation. Strikingly architectural trees, from yuccas to screw pines, cabbage palms to African tulip trees, create a framework for technicolour tropical flowers, from hibiscus and bougainvillea to giant begonias and birds of paradise. Between, pockets of lawn open out to vast views across the northern hills. The Flower Forest is open daily 09:00–17:00, Highway 2, Richmond Plantation, St Joseph, tel: 433 8152, www.flower-forestbarbados.com

North of Mount Hillaby, the 30ha (74-acre) **Turner's Hall Wood** is the only surviving pocket of the indigenous woodland that once smothered the island, with some 100 species of trees and plants, including silk cotton, beef wood, and Spanish oak trees.

8
The North

The parishes of St Peter, on the west coast, St Andrew on the east and St Lucy at the top make up the relatively undeveloped north of Barbados. Here the gentle white sand beaches give way to cliffs and coves. This is the highest point of the island, the tiny volcanic fragment forced up on its end to act as a peg from which to hang the coral reefs, a lush landscape of sugar fields, rambling villages, vegetable patches and fruit orchards wrapped around tiny patches of dense forest.

Speightstown

Heading north on Highway 1, the yellow rasta bus belting out reggae hits, you could easily miss the best of **Speightstown**. Named after William Speight, a member of the first Barbados Assembly and the original owner of the land on which the settlement stands, it was marked on early maps as Spyke's Bay and has been pronounced Spikestown since its earliest years. The second largest town on the island, it was a whaling station and the colony's major port, commercial and slaving centre until the development of Bridgetown, picking up the nickname 'Little Bristol' because of the regular ships calling here on the triangular route between Bristol, in England, the Gold Coast in West Africa (picking up slaves), and the West Indies (dropping off slaves and picking up sugar).

In 1649, when Cromwell sent out a force to quell royalist dissidents on the island (*see page 15*), his troops tried for a full six months to take the town but were fought off at every attempt, eventually taking the island only when they landed

> ## DON'T MISS
>
> ** **Speightstown:** quaint colonial architecture.
> ** **Little Bay:** wild waves.
> * **Barbados Wildlife Reserve:** monkeying around.
> * **North Point:** vast views of the ocean blue.
> * **Morgan Lewis Sugar Mill:** wind power for a sugar rush.

◄ *Opposite: The rocks of Little Bay produce spectacular spray as waves crash into and through the cliffs.*

THE NORTH

▲ *Above: Speightstown has some of Barbados's oldest surviving architecture.*

at Oistins on the south coast. The remains of **Denmark** and **Orange forts** still stand in the town centre and a few old cannons line the **Esplanade**, but none of the other 17th-century structures have survived the inevitable fires. Nevertheless, Speightstown boasts the best-preserved historic district on the island, its narrow streets lined by the overhanging galleries of 18th-century townhouses, best seen along **Queen Street**, **Church Street** and **Orange Street**. The grandest of the townhouses, **Arlington House** is now an interactive museum (open Mon–Sat 09:00–17:00, tel: 422 4064).

St Peter's Parish Church has stood here since 1629, although the present Greek revival building dates to 1837 and was rebuilt after a fire in 1980. Many of the old houses were nearly derelict before recent restoration projects injected new life. A good collection of shops, cafés and restaurants, a modern mall and busy weekend market stalls make the little town popular with locals and tourists alike. Drop into one of the best galleries in the Caribbean, the **Gallery of Caribbean Art** in the Northern Business Centre (open Monday–Friday 09:30–16:30, Saturday 09:30–14:00, tel: 419 0858, www.artgallerycaribbean.com), before settling down with a beer and a plate of flying fish at the **Fisherman's Pub**. Art lovers will also appreciate the vast (80 x 20ft) "trompe l'oeil" mural which covers the side of the building overlooking L'Attitude Restaurant. Commissioned by restaurateur, Pierre Spenard, it is the work of Californian artists John and Annie Pugh and Barbadian artist, Don Small and shows the island's tourist highlights in gloriously clever 3D effect. To work off the effects, take a long walk along the National Trust's guided **Arbib Nature and Heritage Trail**

THE CAROLINAS CONNECTION

It was planters from Barbados, led by Sir John Colleson, who first colonized Charleston, South Carolina, in 1670 and the two colonies kept close ties right up to the American War of Independence. Many of the houses in Speightstown are architecturally very similar to the Charleston 'single' houses (with one gable, one large commercial room downstairs, living quarters upstairs), which were built with a veranda along one side of the house, back to front, to catch as much of the breeze as possible.

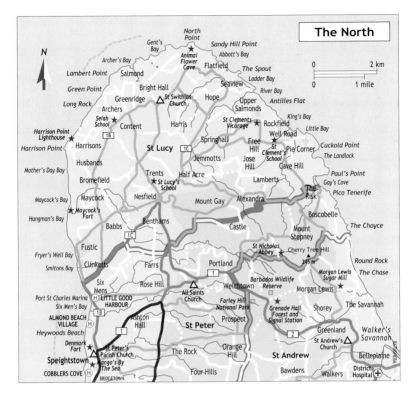

(tours daily 09:30 and 14:30; book at least four days in advance;
tel: 426 2421, http://barbadosnationaltrust.org). The trail lasts
four hours and is not for children under five. This is only one of
a number of hiking and outdoor activities offered by the local
National Trusts including eco-adventures at sea, moonlight walks
and camping trips (see also page 101).

THE NORTH COAST

Just to the north of town, the line of magnificent west-coast
beaches continues through **Heywoods Beach**, home of the
huge Almond Beach Village resort (see page 114), with a
ruined sugar mill in its grounds. The Speightstown fishing
boats give way to sleek gin palaces at the ultra-luxurious,

THE NORTH

environmentally friendly **Port St Charles Marina**, the carefully gated moorings surrounded by chic apartments for the financially overloaded. It even has its own immigration and customs office, where those who wish to enter the island by yacht can dock and be processed screened from prying paparazzi. It was while digging foundations for the development that workmen uncovered archaeological evidence that pushed the inhabited history of the island back to around 4000 years ago (2000 years further than previously imagined).

Beyond this, **Little Good Harbour** and **Six Men's Bay** are losing a rearguard action against the developers but, for the moment, are some of the few places on the west coast where you will still find local fishing communities, with a fine fish market, rum shops, hotly contested games of dominoes, and a smaller version of the Oistins famous Friday night fish fry. Beyond here, as the cliff rears upwards from the sea, Maycock's Bay is reached only down the steep paths to **Maycock's Fort** and the **Harrison Point Lighthouse**.

NORTH POINT AND SURROUNDS

Carry on right up to the north of the island for a view off the cliffs of … absolutely nothing but sea – the Caribbean to the left and the Atlantic to the right. This is where you really get a sense of quite how isolated this tiny island is. Beneath the viewing point, a small, dank staircase leads down into the **Animal Flower Cave**. In here, the mouth of the vast limestone

▼ *Below: Little Bay doesn't have fine sand, but it is one of the prettiest and least visited spots on the coast.*

cavern frames the pounding surf but there are sadly few signs these days of the once dramatic sea anemones and tube worms that gave the cave its name. Open daily 09:00–17:00, tel: 439 8797, www.facebook.com/animalflowercave

Around the corner, on the east coast, the wild cliffs and crashing waves continue, broken by small coves such as the aptly named **River Bay**, a very popular

▲ *Above: St Nicholas Abbey is one of only three Jacobean mansions in the Americas.*

local picnic spot; **Little Bay**, its cliff sporting a funky doughnut hole in the rock; and **Cove Bay**, officially known as Gay's Cove, with its headland, **Paul's Point**. South of this, the spiky 80m (262ft) **Pico Tenerife** gazes across 3000km (1864 miles) of open water to the next landfall, Tenerife in the Canary Islands.

The best view of this coast can be found about 4km (2.5 miles) further south and a little way inland, through Boscobelle village, from the top of 245m (804ft) **Cherry Tree Hill**, with its superb avenue of mahogany trees.

St Nicholas Abbey

On the far side of Cherry Tree Hill, the route is lined by a magnificent 550m (1805ft) avenue of mahogany trees – with not a cherry in sight – leading down to St Nicholas Abbey. This is one of only three Jacobean (early 17th-century) houses in the entire Western hemisphere. The others are Drax Hall (*see* page 76) and Bacon's Castle, Virginia, USA. In spite of its name, it never was an abbey or anything to do with the church, and was named after one of its owners, George Nicholas, who married Susannah, the granddaughter of its founder (the 'St' and 'Abbey' got tacked on in the 19th century, presumably for snob appeal). Typically English in design, it was built by Colonel Benjamin Berringer in the 1650s. He was killed in a duel by his business partner, Sir John Yeamans, who promptly married the widow and moved in. In 1669, Berringer's children

MAHOGANY

First introduced to Barbados from Africa by John Henry Barrow in the 1780s, mahogany is not indigenous to the island but has thrived here. With most of the original forest decimated for building, firewood and clearance by the early settlers, much of the island's remaining forest has a large proportion of mahogany while its wood is valued for furniture and crafts.

eventually reclaimed their father's property and the errant couple moved to South Carolina, where Yeamans helped found the colony of which he eventually became governor. From then on, St Nicholas Abbey was passed down through the family, until 1816 when it was bought by the Cummerbatch brothers, whose descendants still live here. Throughout, it remained one of the richest sugar plantations on the island. An inventory in 1834 showed the estate to be worth £55,974, the amount including 407 acres at £50 an acre and 184 slaves, worth £60 each.

Today, the magnificent mansion, with its row of Dutch gables, carved coral stone finials and corner chimneys, is open to the public, having recently undergone extensive and much-needed restoration. As well as having the opportunity to explore the ground floor of this magnificent house (still a family home), you can watch a fascinating historic movie about life on a sugar plantation in the 1930s and see the lovingly restored steam sugar mill (which

▼ Below: Morgan Lewis Sugar Mill is the island's last working windmill, grinding cane once a month for the tourists during the cutting season.

operates on high days and holidays) and rum distillery. Add to this the beautiful gardens, exotic trees, Moluccan cockatoos, a chance to taste the rum, have a meal and shop. Open Sun–Fri 10:00–15:30, tel: 422 8725, www.st nicholasabbey.com

Morgan Lewis Sugar Mill

Head back over Cherry Tree Hill and follow the road south to the island's only fully working sugar mill – and the only fully work-ing sugar mill in the world – restored and run by the

National Trust. For centuries, the entire industry was wind-powered and every plantation had its own mill. The Morgan Lewis mill was built in 1727 and worked right through to 1945. The ideal time to visit is on the few days during the sugar season when it is working, but even if you can't manage that, it is still well worth a stop to admire the mill itself, explore the ruined plantation home and browse through the little museum of photos and equipment used in sugar production. There are also wonderful views from the hill over farmlands, sea and the wild, windswept Morgan Lewis Beach. The mill is open Monday–Friday 09:00–17:00; milling one Sunday a month, from February to June, tel: 422 7429, http://barbadosnationaltrust.org

▲ *Above: Grenade Hall Signal Station sporting the French tricouleur.*

Barbados Wildlife Reserve

Carry on down the road and turn west onto Highway 2 and you reach a side turning up to the **Barbados Wildlife Reserve** on Farley Hill, St Peter. This is more a zoo than a reserve, particularly given the island's severe shortage of indigenous wildlife, but it still makes for an entertaining and informative afternoon and is great for children. Set in the midst of mahogany forests, there are no dangerous animals here and you just stroll the paths looking for the remarkably well-camouflaged inhabitants as you go. Remember that they are not tame and should not be touched. Is that rock really a rock or one of a positive army of huge tortoises? The rustle in the leaves is actually a grazing red brocket deer. The weird-looking oversized rabbit on stilts is a Patagonian mara, the miniature dinosaur an iguana. There are hundreds of birds, from parrots to pelicans, flamingos and finches in a walk-through aviary and some safely caged caimans and snakes,

BARBADOS GREEN MONKEYS

The Barbados green monkey is not indigenous to the island – nor is it green, although the fur is said to have a slightly olive-green tinge. They are, in fact, native to Gambia and Senegal in West Africa and were imported around 350 years ago, evolving since into a separate subspecies. They generally live in troops of about 15. There are estimated to be up to 10,000 on the island, although they are shy and rarely seen outside the Wildlife Reserve.

mainly pythons and boas. The undoubted stars, however, are the green monkeys (see panel, this page) that live wild, swinging through the trees and keeping well out of the way of people until lunchtime. The downside of the Wildlife Reserve is that it is linked to the Barbados Primate Research Centre which uses the island's monkeys for medical re-search, and exports them to other labs around the world. Try to time your visit to see them come down to be fed at 14:00 every day. Open daily 10:00–17:00 (last admission 16:00), tel: 422 8826.

Literally across the car park are the **Grenade Hall Forest and Signal Station**. Take the path on the left up the hill to the signal station, built in 1819 as part of a series of stations across the island designed to give planters a quick warning of any slave rebellion. The uprising led by Bussa three years before had resulted in widespread violence, with 176 killed during the fighting and 214 slaves executed. It also fanned the flames of the abolition movement. Next time, the plantation owners would be ready. The station now contains a small display on the uprising and the island's six signal stations. For an island that prides itself on never having been French, it also flies a French flag! Needless to say, it also offers wonderful views.

Back in the car park, a network of nature trails leads down through the dense **Grenade Hall Forest**. Much of it is mahogany trees, but there are small patches of indigenous trees and plenty of smaller plants. Apart from the delights of the shady trails themselves, monkeys range free around here and there's a chance for some bird-watching. The signs are also excellent, identifying species and offering explana-tions of the plants' various medicinal uses.

▼ *Below: Thousands turn out for concerts in the Barbados Jazz Festival.*

Farley Hill National Park

Back on the main road, only a few metres on, a turning leads off to Farley Hill. Originally built by Sir Graham Briggs in 1818 but massively extended in 1857, it was, without peer, the island's grandest mansion, surrounded by magnificent botanic gardens. For nearly a century, a steady stream of celebrity visitors including royalty gathered in the home that was described by the English historian James Anthony Froude as 'a palace with which Aladdin himself might have been satisfied'. In 1956, it provided the location for the Harry Belafonte movie, *Island in the Sun*. Nine years later, it was definitively destroyed by fire. It was decided not to rebuild and in 1967 the ruin in wooded parkland rich in fruit trees became a national park. It is now one of the islanders' favourite picnic spots, with plenty of shade, pleasant strolls and fine views over the Scotland District. It's also popular for weddings and is a major arts venue, with open-air concerts during the Barbados Jazz Festival and Gospelfest.

▲ *Above: Farley Hill, ruined by a massive fire in 1964, is now a mere shadow of its former glory.*

9
What to do in Barbados

One of the joys of this tiny island is that everything is accessible in under an hour's drive, no matter where you stay. There are plenty of sights, but many of the most popular tourist activities are nationwide.

HIGHLIGHTS

For the sake of easy navigation, the highlights are listed in strict alphabetical order.

Buying a Home

If, like many, the idea of buying a house and settling on Barbados is appealing, be prepared to spend serious amounts of money. A chattel house inland will be expensive; even a relatively humble west-coast villa will set you back several million US$. The political stability of Barbados – let alone its lively social scene, tropical climate and beaches – makes it a popular choice. Anyone planning to live permanently in Barbados must prove to the government's Immigration Department that they will not become a burden on the island's taxpayers. Documents showing applicants' ability to support themselves must be given to the Chief Immigration Officer at Careenage House, The Wharf, Bridgetown. In terms of buying or renting a home, much the same laws of supply and demand exist as they do for the cost of hotels on the island. The west coast is invariably more expensive than the south or the wilder east coast. Anyone trying to buy or rent a home will find that the phone books, the streets of Bridgetown and business

DON'T MISS

*** *Atlantis* submarine: a porthole on an entirely different world.
*** Swimming with turtles: touching ancient magic.
** 4x4 Safari: a day out in the country.
** Race days: it's definitely a good bet!
** Cricket: the second national religion.

◀ *Opposite: If you have a spare hour, why not try dinghy sailing off Dover Beach?*

WHAT TO DO IN BARBADOS

websites are positively crammed with estate agents offering million-pound villas or much humbler homes. Finding providers for ancillary services, like architects and builders, is equally easy, although choosing firms with the best reputations requires the same common sense it would in any other part of the world.

Cricket

Cricket is a religion in Barbados ... although that might be an understatement. The first known reference to cricket on the island was in a newspaper report in 1806, although it's likely that the game was played by soldiers of the British garrison well before that. Barbados hosted the first inter-colony cricket match in 1865 when Guyana were thrashed at the Garrison Savannah by a whites-only Bajan side. Great players of the past, such as Sir Gary Sobers, Frank Worrell, Everton Weekes, Clyde Walcott and Gordon Greenidge, were all Barbadians. The island is a world capital of cricket and its epicentre is the **Kensington Oval**. And while the Oval underwent major refurbishment for the 2007

▼ *Below: An afternoon of cricket in Queen's Park.*

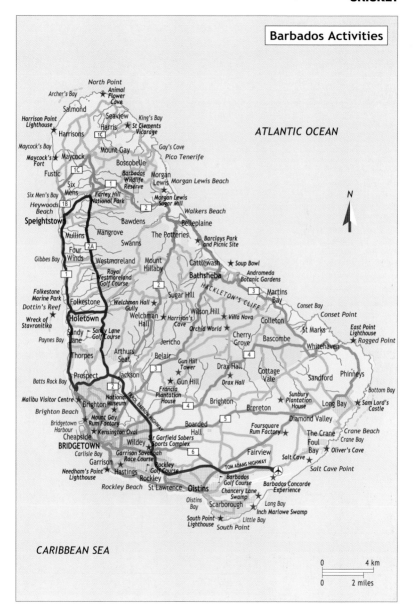

Barbados Activities

ATLANTIC OCEAN

North Point
Animal Flower Cave
Archer's Bay
Salmond
Harrison Point Lighthouse
Seaview
King's Bay
Harris
St Clements Vicarage
Harrisons
1C
Maycock's Bay
Mount Gay
Gay's Cove
Maycock's Fort
Maycock
Pico Tenerife
Boscobelle
Fustic
1C
Barbados Wildlife Reserve
Morgan Lewis
Morgan Lewis Beach
Six Mens
1
Six Men's Bay
Farley Hill National Park
Morgan Lewis Sugar Mill
Heywoods Beach
1B
Walkers Beach
Speightstown
Belleplaine
Mullins
Bawdens
The Potteries
Mangrove
Barclays Park and Picnic Site
Swanns
Four Winds
2A
Gibbes Bay
Westmoreland
Mount Hillaby
Cattlewash
Soup Bowl
Royal Westmoreland Golf Course
2
Bathsheba
Andromeda Botanic Gardens
Folkestone Marine Park
Welchman Hall Gully
Sugar Hill
HACKLETON'S CLIFF
3
Martins Bay
Conset Bay
Dottin's Reef
Folkestone
Welchman Hall
Wilson Hill
Conset Point
Wreck of Stavronikita
Holetown
Harrison's Cave
Villa Nova
Colleton
East Point Lighthouse
Sandy Lane
Sandy Lane Golf Course
Orchid World
St Marks
Ragged Point
Paynes Bay
Jericho
Cherry Grove
Bascombe
Whitehaven
Thorpes
Arthurs Seat
Belair
Gun Hill Tower
4
Prospect
3
Jackson
Gun Hill
Drax Hall
Cottage Vale
Sandford
Phinneys
Batts Rock Bay
2
Francia Plantation House
Drax Hall
Bottom Bay
Malibu Visitor Centre
National Museum
4
Brighton
Brereton
Sunbury Plantation House
Long Bay
Sam Lord's Castle
Brighton Beach
Bridgetown Harbour
Mount Gay Rum Factory
Boarded Hall
Diamond Valley
Cheapside
Kensington Oval
Wildey
5
Foursquare Rum Factory
The Crane
Crane Beach
BRIDGETOWN
Sir Garfield Sobers Sports Complex
Fairview
Foul Bay
Crane Bay
Garrison
Garrison Savannah Race Course
6
TOM ADAMS HIGHWAY
Salt Cave
Oliver's Cave
Carlisle Bay
Rockley Golf Course
Salt Cave Point
Needham's Point Lighthouse
Hastings
Rockley
Barbados Golf Course
Barbados Concorde Experience
Rockley Beach
St Lawrence
Oistins
Chancery Lane Swamp
Oistins Bay
Long Bay
South Point Lighthouse
Scarborough
Inch Marlowe Swamp
South Point
Little Bay

ERROL BARROW HIGHWAY

N

CARIBBEAN SEA

0 ——— 4 km

0 ——— 2 miles

WHAT TO DO IN BARBADOS

cricket World Cup final, it is the village cricket pitches around Barbados – often with a rum shop close by – that offer the best way to experience Bajan cricket. Spend an hour or two on the boundary of a village cricket pitch with a cold beer in your hand watching the graceful skills of Bajan cricketers and, if you're lucky, they may invite you to join in. For listings, *see* page 119.

Dinner Shows

There is no simpler way to dip into the varied music and dance culture of Barbados than to take in a dinner show at the **Harbour Lights** nightclub on Bay Street in St Michael (*see* page 118). Every Monday and Wednesday evening warms up with steel pan music while visitors dine on the barbecue and dance on the sand under the stars. Next up is a fire eater and stilt walker, and then, as the rum flows, comes limbo dancing under a flaming bar. Visitors committed to getting 'interactive' can take the limbo challenge. Jugglers set the tone for a dance show that goes back to the African origins of the slave population, through the early days of Bridgetown and on to Barbados's 'Crop Over Festival'.

▶ *Right: Harbour Lights dedicates itself to serious partying, with live music into the early hours of the morning.*

The producers claim it's the best way for tourists to dip their toes into Caribbean culture (*see also* page 58).

Diving

Barbados claims that it has the clearest, most accessible diving waters in the Caribbean. A number of companies offer dive training and dives for qualified visitors. **Barbados Blue**, based at the Hilton Hotel on the southwest tip of Barbados, is the only facility on the island with two on-staff marine biologists, and also claims that the Hilton beach is the densest hawksbill turtle nesting beach on Barbados, guaranteeing a turtle encounter during a dive. The company offers night dives, drift and deep dives, as well as specialist naturalist and photo dives. Further up the west coast, **West Side Scuba** dives out of Holetown, using four different shipwrecks and two marine parks. Visitors can choose between 20 different reef dive locations and experienced divers are permitted into the hull of the ship *Stavronikita*. For visitors wanting to dive from the north of the island, **Reefers and Wreckers** is based in Speightstown. For listings, *see* page 119.

WHAT A DIVE!

Amongst the island's finest dive sites is the dome-shaped Bell Buoy reef (6.5–20m/ 21–66ft), with brown coral tree forests and large schools of fish; Dottin's Reef (12–20m/ 39–66ft), off Holetown, where you can find schooling fish, barracudas, and turtles; Maycock's Bay, on the northwest coast, where the reefs are separated by white sand, and visibility is crystal clear; and Silver Bank, with healthy coral, fish and sea fans. Artificial reefs have grown up around the wrecked freighter *Pamir* (18m/59ft) off Six Men's Bay; the freighter *Stavronikita* (41m/135ft), and in Carlisle Bay near Bridgetown where there are seven shipwrecks (*Berwyn, Fox, CTrek, Friar's Crag, Eilon*, the barge *Cornwallis*, and *Bajan Queen*).

◄ *Left: A scuba diver explores a coral reef off the west coast.*

4x4 Safaris

Four-wheel-drive Jeep and Land Rover safaris are one of the liveliest ways of touring Barbados. The very nature of the vehicles means you get far off the beaten track – often no more than 100m (109yd) from the nearest tarred road, but who cares! On simpler tours, visitors are driven through the centre of the island and to the quieter north and east coasts, calling at main tourist attractions, such as Gun Hill and Welchman Hall Gully gardens, taking to farm tracks where possible. These usually include a buffet lunch.
Island Safari (tel: 429 5337, www.islandsafari.bb)

Game Fishing

Ever fancied yourself as Hemingway, wrestling with a gleaming, fighting fish from the back of a shiny yacht? Now's your chance, with plenty of charter boats attracting

▶ *Opposite: Bringing home a dolphin fish after a morning's game fishing.*

▼ *Below: Island Safari do their best to make you believe the beaten track isn't right next door. It may not be all that adventurous, but it's a great day out.*

novices and seasoned hunters alike during the season (mid-November to May). You won't have far to go. Barbados's underwater geography means that water depths fall to more than 120m (394ft) within 1.5km (1 mile) of the shore, while the 500m (1640ft) contour is as close as 5km (3 miles) from the island. Fish targeted during the season include white marlin, dorado, sailfish, wahoo, yellow-fin tuna and blue marlin; the latter have reached a record 230kg (505lb) in these waters. The **Barbados Game Fishing Association** (PO Box 80, Bridgetown, Barbados, tel: 428 6668, http://barbadosgamefishing.com) runs formal tournaments

through the year. Visitors can take part as long as they give sufficient advance notice and pay a fee. They will also provide complete contacts with charter companies (e-mail: secretary@barbadosgamefishing.com). There are tournaments for specific fish, such as barracuda, google eye and wahoo, and Barbados also hosts an international game-fishing tournament at the end of March every year.

Leading companies include **IOU Charters** (tel: 269 8905, www.iouchartersbarbados.net), which operates a 36ft, twin-diesel Sportfisher boat and is British captained; **Cannon Charters** (tel: 424 6107, www.fishingbarbados.com); and **High Seas Barbados Fishing Charters** (tel: 233 2598, http://sportfishingbarbados.com).

DOLPHIN FISH

Not to be confused with the dolphin, the dolphin fish (*Coryphaena hippurus*) – otherwise known as the mahi-mahi or dorado – is a game fish commonly found in Barbadian waters and on the island's plates. They are not huge, averaging 7–13kg (15–29lb), although the largest can be three times that weight. Respected by sportsmen as ferocious fighters, they grow fast, swim fast and are carnivorous.

WHAT TO DO IN BARBADOS

GOLF GOES TECHIE

The Barbados Golf Club has a 6805yd par 72 course. Rockley Golf and Country Club is a nine-hole par 70, 5610yd. At Sandy Lane, both the Country Club (7060yd, par 74.7) and the Green Monkey courses (reserved for resort guests) were designed by Tom Fazio. The Royal Westmoreland's 6870yd par 70 course is the brainchild of Robert Trent Jones Jr.

▼ Below: Sandy Lane golf course was home to the 2006 WGC World Golf Championship, won by German team Bernhard Langer and Marcel Siem.

Golf

The Caribbean climate – and the balmy breezes in particular – make golf a perfect pastime for people in Barbados, provided of course you have the basic golfing skills. The island currently has three 18-hole golf courses with two other full courses under development. Wealthy golfers with resident status head to either the **Royal Westmoreland** (www.royal-westmoreland.com) or **Sandy Lane** (www.sandylane.com/golf), which has public access (a second Sandy Lane course is reserved for residents only). Visitors wanting a round with cheaper green fees should head for the **Barbados Golf Club** (www.barbadosgolf-club.com) at Durants in Christ Church. There are also two nine-hole courses – one at the **Rockley Golf and Country Club** (http://rockleygolfclub.com) and the 'old nine' at Sandy Lane – and a golf academy with driving range and a chip-and-putt par three at the **Almond Beach Village**. There are a number of golfing and hotel packages suggested on the tourist office website, www.barbados.org/barbados_golf_vacations.php

GOLF, GO TO THE MOVIES, HORSE RACING, HOCKEY & RUGBY

Go to the Movies

Take a trip back to 1950s small town USA at the **Globe Drive-In Cinema**, Adam's Castle, Christ Church, tel: 437 0480 on the South Coast. There are three shows a night, films change weekly, there's plenty of popcorn and hotdogs and you set your car radio for sound and sit back and wallow in nostalgia. For indoor movies with style, try the **Limegrove Cinema**, Limegrove Lifestyle Centre, Holetown, tel: 271 0071, http://www.limegrovecinemas.com on the West Coast where you get waitress service at your seat and can nosh as you watch.

Hockey and Rugby

Hockey and rugby are increasingly popular team sports on Barbados. The **Banks Beer International Hockey Festival** in late August every year is the biggest in the western hemisphere and attracts teams from across the globe. Men's, women's and veterans' events are held on the immaculate Astroturf surface at the Sir Garfield Sobers sports complex. Rugby Barbados has been internationally recognized since 1995 and has three senior teams on the island, which play at the Garrison Savannah and welcome touring sides and individual rugby players on the island. **Barbados Hockey Federation** (tel: 428 9834, www.barbadoshockey.org); **Barbados Rugby Football Union** (tel: 437 3838, www.rugby-barbados.com).

Horse Racing

The Garrison Savannah racecourse, less than 3km (2 miles) from the centre of Bridgetown, has been the centre of island horse racing since 1845. British army officers stationed on Barbados created the six-furlong grass oval around the military parade ground to exercise and race their mounts. Nowadays the Barbados Turf Club, founded in 1905, organizes three different seasons of racing each year. The seasons run from January to April, May to August, and October to December. The biggest races in the calendar are the **Sandy Lane Gold Cup**, the **Banks Barbados Guineas**, the **Midsummer Creole Classic** and the **Barbados Derby**. The

> ### CHERRY RIPE
>
> Indigenous to the island, the Barbados cherry (*Malpighia emarginata*) bears small, bright red fruit with a massive concentration of vitamin C and was traditionally used to treat sore throats, coughs and colds, liver ailments, diarrhoea and dysentery. It also tastes good: raw, as jam or with ice cream.

WHAT TO DO IN BARBADOS

A DAY AT THE RACES

However serious you may be about a day at the races, some gambling and seeing the horses tear round the Garrison Savannah track, be sure not to miss the pervasive atmosphere of fun on a major race day. There are parades of marching bands, mounted police, stilt walkers, all the fun of the fair inside the track, while wealthy and poor locals gather around the perimeter for parties that continue well into the night. Everyone is welcome.

Turf Club runs races just for Barbados-bred horses and for animals from the wider West Indies. A dress code operates for the grandstand and for the clubhouse, but in the outfield locals and tourists mingle and enjoy the racing free of such restrictions. Food stalls sell a variety of takeaway snacks, such as fried fish, fishcakes and 'pudding and *souse*'. Most stalls are licensed for rum and beer. Entry to the grandstand costs very little but prices rise on the most prestigious race days. Younger children can be kept happy at a play park. A race day at the Garrison Savannah is likely to be one of the most memorable parts of a Barbados stay (*see also* page 51). For listings, *see* page 119.

Zipping along

The **Aerial Trek Zipline Adventure** (Jack-in-the-Box Gully, Walkes Spring, St Thomas, tel: 438 8735, www.aerialtrek.com) is an amazing attraction for the fairly fit (over 12 years and under 250lb). Roped up, you are zipped in a sort of bosun's chair between eight platforms through the canopies of the trees, seeing the world from a whole new and thrilling angle. Tour guides explain the eco-system as you go.

Marriage

The idea of saying your vows in a flower-decked gazebo

▼ Below: Have a flutter on the horses at the Barbados Turf Club and you may just pay for your holiday.

just feet from the lapping Caribbean exercises a powerful draw on the imaginations of couples from colder corners of the world. Getting married in Barbados is not a complicated business. There is no legal minimum residency requirement, but a marriage licence must be obtained from the authorities. Both parties must apply

▲ *Above: Ziplining is a great way to see the views from a different perspective.*

in person at the Ministry of Home Affairs in Bridgetown. Applications must be made with passports or birth certificates and return tickets to leave the island. There are further legal requirements in the case of divorcees or widows. Roman Catholics have to contact the bishop of Bridgetown. The licence costs is US$100, with a further local and smaller stamp fee. Couples must be sure to arrange a minister of religion or a civil magistrate personally or through a wedding planner. Idyllic beachside locations are offered by any number of hotels and commercial wedding planning companies, most of which also offer a range of even more exotic locations at plantation great houses, orchid farms or on yachts. Wedding extras include photography, musicians, beauticians and public-address systems. While you could do it all yourself, it is strongly advised that you consult a local to ensure that you get the legal requirements straight.

A good starting point is with the list on the tourist office website, www.barbados.org/weddings.htm

National Trust Walks

For the last 30 years, the Barbados National Trust (*see* page 50) has been organizing guided walks to the less well-known corners of the island. Hikes last from around three hours and to combat the tropical climate they usually leave at 06:00 or in mid-afternoon and always on Sundays. Visitors are advised to check the kind of terrain they'll be covering because some walks have been described as 'not for sissies'. The

PRIDE OF BARBADOS

A large shrub, growing up to 5m (16ft) tall although often cultivated as a hedge, the dwarf poinciana or flower fence (*Poinciana pulcherrima*) is the national flower of the island. Blooming year-round, it has small flowers of fiery orange/red and a yellow frill. It was first mentioned in 1657 and appears on the national coat of arms, which also shows the bearded fig tree, a dolphin fish, a pelican and the motto 'Pride and Industry'.

WHAT TO DO IN BARBADOS

▲ *Above: Hikers admire the view from Hackleton's Cliff, before the long climb back down to the coast.*

toughest category is 'grin and bear', which can cover 20–30km (12–19 miles); 'here and there' can range up to 16km (10 miles). Some are gentler and described as 'stop and stare'. On those walks you'll generally find a more sociable, chatty atmosphere from your guide and also from fellow walkers. The **Hike Barbados** (tel: 230 4818, www.hikebarbados.com) programme could take a visitor through sugar-cane fields, gullies, tropical forest and coastal villages to explore the unique geology of Barbados. Tourists who join the hikes say it's virtually impossible not to make good friends among local island walkers. The Barbados National Trust does not make a formal charge for the walks but donations are welcomed. If your schedule doesn't allow you to join the public walk, you can also book a hiking guide for a three-, six-, eight- or 10-mile hike, personalized to your own needs.

Open Houses and Gardens

There is always a temptation to peek behind closed doors and it is especially compelling if the homes in question are fine historic properties. Many homes contain rare colonial mahogany furniture, period ornaments and art and sculpture. Evergreen in Sandy Lane is an airily elegant neoclassical villa with its own Caribbean features, such as exterior walls that fold open to let the breeze in. Cluffs Plantation House in St Lucy has been lovingly restored to its 18th-century condition. It contains furniture collected from almost every other great house on the island. The Barbados National Trust's **Open House** programme helps the public and visitors to peer behind the doors of these and other private homes ranging from the historic treasures of plantation great houses to simple but typical chattel homes in which slaves once lived. Tours are on Wednesday afternoons from January to April, and begin promptly at 14:30. Visitors are strongly advised not to turn up at a property any earlier than the official time – home-owners get fed up with their day being disturbed. On Saturdays, it is the turn of the gardens, the programme organized by the **Barbados Horticultural Society** (tel: 428 5889). Details from the **Barbados National Trust**, Wildey, St Michael, tel: 426 2421, www.barbadosnationaltrust.org

Party Boats

Visitors looking for some old-fashioned fun out on the Caribbean itself have a variety of choices, from the risqué, boozy *Jolly Roger* pirate cruise to offerings that are more sophisticated. The spacious ***Harbour Master*** has room for 700 guests on its four decks and offers a style that can be loosely described as 'corporate entertainment'. It serves lunch and dinner at sea. Complete with pirate-themed entertainment, including rope-

◀ *Left: The* Jolly Roger *lives up to its name: it's a real party ship where the rum flows freely.*

swinging into the water and a mock pirate wedding, the **Jolly Roger** is well recognized as the endearingly rowdy option as it takes its lunchtime and evening cruise up the west coast from Bridgetown. The **Rubáiyát** is a 50ft catamaran that offers lunch and dinner cruises for smaller, quieter groups. **Tiami Catamarans** has a fleet of five boats and its five-hour lunchtime cruises begin with champagne cocktails. The crew sails gently up the west coast, stopping for guests to swim and snorkel, and plies everyone with drinks as they go. Most of the boats offering party cruises stop somewhere along the west coast to allow passengers to swim with the turtles, or choose their own water sports. When vessels stop they are invariably surrounded by a flotilla of waterbikes trying to sell their high-speed thrills. The boats all leave from Shallow Draught harbour in Bridgetown or The Careenage. For listings, *see* page 119.

▼ *Below: Polo teams from across the globe visit Barbados to battle it out over rum punch.*

Polo

Polo in Barbados is undergoing some challenging times after the island's women's team defeated the men! It's

a far cry from the old days, when polo was first played officially in Barbados in 1927. Polo is played during the winter season from the end of December through to late April. There are four fields on the island – at Holders and Waterhall in St James, and at Clifton and Lion Castle in St Thomas. Lion Castle's 4.5ha (11-acre) field and clubhouse complex is surrounded by a luxury housing development. Apart from Barbados's own teams, international polo players visit every year from the UK, South Africa, Argentina, Mexico and several polo-playing areas in the southern USA. The **Barbados Open** is the most important date on the island's polo calendar, but smaller, more traditional competitions featuring local teams are equally enthusiastically supported. Package holidays, including polo tuition and matches, are available from Sovereign Holidays in the UK. Packages are tailored to the polo handicap needs of holiday-makers and include flights, villa or hotel, morning training sessions, the use of a horse and participation in a polo match. **Barbados Polo Club** (tel: 432 1802, http://barbadospoloclub.com); **Lion Castle** (tel: 432 0840, www.lioncastlepoloestate.com).

Racing
See Horse Racing on page 100.

Rallying
Motor enthusiasts have been rallying here for the last 45 years and the sport is popular on Barbados even though the country is only 430km² (166 sq miles) in size. Barbados has organized and hosted internationally acclaimed special-stage rallies since 1988. While drivers are expected not to drink, the year's main event is the **Barbados Rally Carnival** (www.barbadosrallycarnival.com) with all the off-road fun that the name suggests. The dense network of paved roads is especially suited for tarmac rallies, and the facilities include a RallySprint track at Vaucluse Raceway, built in 2000.

Rugby
See Hockey and Rugby on page 99.

Running

An early morning jog along the beach or through the cane fields is the stuff of magic. For marathon and other long-distance runners, **Run Barbados** is a series of different distance events every December. Full marathons and even shorter events begin at 05:00. The motto of Run Barbados is quite clear when it says, 'Come for the run – stay for the fun'. **Run Barbados** (tel: 467 3600, www.runbarbados.org); **Hash Harriers** (tel: 420 8113, www.barbadoshash.com).

Sailing

One of the pleasures of Barbados is the free sailing visitors can enjoy from many hotels, but particularly from the more expensive west-coast hotels. For wealthier tourists it's usually just a case of telling the water-sports desk when you want to relax on the Hobie Cat's netting and the booking is made. And even where hotels themselves don't provide the simpler dinghy sailing free of charge, most beaches have Hobie Cats and other small sailing boats for hire. For the tourist who is thinking a little bigger but still aiming at a half-day sail, there are several companies offering crewed luxury vessels. **Tiami Catamarans**

▼ *Below: A catamaran cruise is a perfect laid-back day out, with swimming, sunshine, snorkelling, great food and good company.*

has five boats offering lunch cruises or sunset cruises. And that's the pattern for most charter companies – two cruises each day. Most include a full buffet lunch and free drinks in their price. The standard offering is also a stop to swim or snorkel on a wreck, swim with turtles and visit a quiet, secluded beach. Other firms worth checking out are **Dreams Catamaran** (www.dreamsbarbados.com/Catamaran), **El Tigre** (*see* page 119), **Heatwave** (www.heatwavesailingcruises.com) and **Silver Moon** (*see* page 119). It is also possible to charter sailing vessels for a number of days – crewed or bare boat – and to cruise around the Windward Islands. Try **Barbados Yacht Club** (tel: 427 1125, www.barbadosyachtclub.com) or **Barbados Sailing Association** (PO Box 40, Bridgetown, www.sailbarbados.com).

Segway Adventure

George Bush managed to fall off a pavement, but in Barbados, the segways have been adapted into sturdier all-terrain affairs for a thoroughly entertaining 90-minute tour of the north of the island from Cove Bay to Little Bay. They are also shortly adding electric bike tours of the island. Segway of Barbados, Bay Street, Bridgetown, tel: 426 5740, www.segwaybarbados.com Tours daily 09:45–11:15, 13:45–15:15.

Submarine Trips

The shadowy turquoise world of the sightseeing submarine is the closest that many will ever get to scuba diving and,

◀ *Left: The* Atlantis *wafts you into a magical turquoise world, the closest non-divers will ever get to the coral reefs.*

WHAT TO DO IN BARBADOS

Along much of the west coast, there are shallow coral reefs just offshore. Sadly most are dead, but the rock can cut your feet and there may be sea urchins or crabs, so tread carefully and wear beach shoes. Be careful never to touch or stand on living coral as it is highly fragile and under threat. On shore, steer clear of the manchineel trees growing on the beach, no matter how tempting their shade may seem. Touching them can cause painfully severe skin rashes and, if you rub your eyes, blindness, while eating the fruit can be deadly.

TURTLES

The most common turtle in Barbados is the relatively small hawksbill turtle, named after its pointed, beak-like nose and jaw. The shell averages 87cm (34 in) long and an average adult weighs about 80kg (176½lb). A newly hatched nestling weighs under 20g (¾oz). They live in coral reefs, living off sponges. They nest between July and October each year, laying several clutches of up to 140 eggs, which take 60 days to hatch. Although on the endangered species list, numbers are continuing to decline.

without doubt, one of the finest activities on the island. The Canadian-built *Atlantis* submarine, based at Shallow Draught harbour, Bridgetown, has now taken more than a million tourists to the base of the coral reef off the island's west coast. The trip (taking over two hours) starts in the shuttle boat, *Ocean Quest*, which ferries you to the submarine moored offshore. Inside the roomy, non-claustrophobic and air-conditioned vessel every tourist has a metre-wide circular window through which to view the fish, corals and the wreck of ship *Lord Willoughby*. The dive itself, to depths of 40–50m (130–165ft), lasts 45 minutes. Dive crew give a running commentary on the flora and fauna of the coral wall and shipwrecks, from moray eels to fragile fan corals.

Be aware, though, that there are restrictions on passengers: disabled people must be able to climb down a seven-step ship's ladder, and children must be at least 1m (3ft) tall. The price structure means cheaper tickets for children under the age of 12 and adult tickets include a free soft drink and a T-shirt. The submarine makes two descents daily and the late afternoon trip, when the *Atlantis's* floodlights are used as daylight fades, usually gives a much brighter, technicolour view of corals.

Atlantis Submarines Barbados (tel: 436 8968, http://barbados.atlantissubmarines.com).

Swim With Turtles

Hawksbill and leatherback turtles live in large numbers along almost all the reefs that protect the south and west coasts of Barbados. The turtle population, though, is greater on the calmer west coast. Decades ago the turtles were endangered by hunting, but are now protected and earn their keep very successfully as a tourist attraction for visitors who take a range of trips to swim with them. There's a plethora of companies operating powered or sailing vessels to reach the turtle habitats. In good weather, tour companies guarantee about an 80 per cent likelihood of finding plenty of animals with which to swim. It's perfectly safe for children and adults to be in the water close to turtles, and tour companies provide snorkelling equipment and life jackets. The only danger is being run down by competitive boats

in the frenzy of activity. Among firms offering turtle swimming experiences are **Tiami Catamarans** (tel: 430 0900, http://tiami-catamarancruises.com), Silver Moon (*see* page 119) and **Thriller Turtle and Shipwreck Snorkel Tour** from Island Safaris (*see* page 118). For visitors who've never snorkelled or dived, **Snuba Scuba** is a novel way of exploring shallow underwater habitats. Snuba divers simply breathe underwater with a 6m (20ft) air line that dangles from an air tank on a raft that follows the divers. Some locations on the west coast are close enough to turtle habitats for strong swimmers to venture out from the shoreline. Less adventurous tourists can take glass-bottomed boat trips and simply view turtles from above (*see also* panels, pages 65 and 108). **Westwater Adventures** (3 Warren Terrace, St Thomas, tel: 421 6008, http://westwater-adventures-barbados.com) offer a range of offshore tours including glass-bottomed boats for those who want to see the dazzling underwater world, but don't want to get wet.

▲ *Above: The local hawksbill turtles are well attuned to humans and happy to swim with the tourists who flock to see them each day.*

Tennis

Tennis is available at most of the best hotels on Barbados, as well as at a number of specialist facilities. The year-round breeze that cools the Windward Islands – and Barbados, which is even further east into the Atlantic – means you don't have to play first thing in the morning or at dusk to avoid the heat. Right across the island there are public tennis courts for hire

WHAT TO DO IN BARBADOS

WAVERIDERS

The water is warm, the sun shines and there are surfing possibilities almost all year and all round the island, but the best time to catch waves is between October and March. Experienced surfers should head to the Soup Bowl on the northeast coast, where waves reach 2–3m (6–10ft) in season and 0.6–2m (2–6ft) the rest of the year. Beginners should head for South Point, where the conditions tend to be kinder to rookie surfers.

▼ Below: The surfboard stays on the beach and the sun block takes over when the sea is millpond calm.

and the **National Tennis Centre** (*see* page 119), sited at the Sir Garfield Sobers Sports Complex at Wildey, in St Michael, provides tuition and courts. The other main centres are at **Club Rockley Resort** and the **West Side Tennis Centre** (tel: 432 2050) at Sunset Crest. **Sandy Lane** has nine hard courts, and there are facilities at the **Hilton Hotel**. There are several annual competitions, including the Barclays Bank junior event, the BMW Challenge and the National Tennis Centre Barbados Futures. **Barbados Lawn Tennis Association** (tel: 427 5300 or 427 5298, www.tennisbarbados.org).

Water Sports

Barbados is teeming with water-sport possibilities whether it's water-skiing, jetskiing, surfing and windsurfing or parasailing. All the wind-powered sports are particularly strong on the island because of its location at the very eastern edge of the Caribbean islands, protruding into the Atlantic. Tourist beaches are constantly patrolled by locals on jetskis and in water-ski boats looking for someone to whom to sell. Most operators of fast boats offer banana boat and tubing trips as

well as water-skiing lessons. Tourists are advised that proper water-skiing lessons are best sought from the bigger water-sport companies. The geography of Barbados determines where the best options are for each different water-based activity. The calmer west coast is ideal for water-skiing, while the breezier south offers quality windsurfing, and the wilder east coast has the best conditions for surfing or extreme windsurfing. The best time of year for windsurfing is when the trade winds blow most consistently – that's from mid-November to the end of June. **Falcon Parasail** (tel: 230 9549, http://www.falconparasailing.com/) offer intrepid guests a chance to soar up to about 500m (1640ft) above the surf. The views of the coast from that height almost distract guests from the sporting side of what they are doing, so be sure to check your insurance before you go and, if necessary, take out additional cover as many standard policies will not cover you for water sports.

▲ *Above: There are plenty of options for water sports, but somehow doing nothing seems so much more enticing.*
▶▶ *Overleaf: The beach at King's Bay.*

BEST TIMES TO VISIT

With 3000 hours of sunshine per year, Barbados's good weather is one of its main draws. The tropical climate is at its best from mid-December to mid-April, when rainfall is low and cooling trade winds alleviate the heat, which can get oppressive during the summer when humidity is high (particularly in September and October). These are also the rainiest months of the hurricane season, which runs from July to November, but as Barbados lies on the edge of the hurricane belt it doesn't see really violent storms more than once every ten years or so. Where to go? Few people choose to stay in Bridgetown itself and there is no accommodation on offer in the centre or north of the island. Each of the coasts has a very distinct feel. The west coast is the 'posh' coast. With its white sands and gentle Caribbean seas, this is home to the island's finest hotels and restaurants and the celebrity mansions. The pace, on the whole, is gentle and rarified. The south coast also has wonderful beaches but they are undoubtedly more lively, noisy and crowded (although not wall-to-wall loungers). This is the place to stay if you are on a more limited budget and/or you like to party. The main clubs are all along here. The east coast faces the Atlantic and is much wilder, its beaches and cliffs dashed by wind and waves, while strong currents swirl through the inshore waters. There is relatively little accommodation here and with the sea unsafe for normal swimming, this is the province of the surfers.

GETTING THERE

See Travel Tips, page 121.

GETTING AROUND

See Transport, Travel Tips, page 123.

WHERE TO STAY

With distances so short, there are few real incentives to stay in town and most visitors prefer to stay and eat in the resort areas along the south and west coasts. This is reflected in the small number of downtown hotels and restaurants worth listing either in Bridgetown itself or in the centre, north and east of the country. With very few exceptions, all the hotels have pools and beachfront, so only those that don't will be mentioned. Most offer a range of water sports, with some options complimentary. Most also either have their own land-sports facilities or will arrange access to tennis courts, golf courses, riding, etc. There are very few good budget hotels in Barbados, although booking a package can bring the cost down considerably, as can travelling out of season. The following price brackets are based on high-season prices:
Luxury: Above US$450 per room per day
Mid-range: US$200–450 per room per day
Inexpensive: Up to US$200 per room per day

BRIDGETOWN
Luxury
Sweetfield Manor, Brittons Hill, St Michael, tel: 429 8356, www.sweetfieldmanor.com Fabulous historic plantation home, 1 mile from Bridgetown, converted to a sybaritic B&B, with gourmet breakfasts, a tropical lagoon pool, and spa.

Mid-range
Barbados Hilton, Needham's Point, St Michael, tel: 426 0200, www.hiltoncaribbean.com A five-star resort hotel at Needham's Point, between the Garrison and the city centre. This is the island's premier business hotel but also caters for the holiday trade, with tennis courts, kids' club, land and water sports.
Island Inn Hotel, Aquatic Gap, Bridgetown 1, Barbados, tel: 436 6393, http://islandinn-barbados.com A 19th century rum store in the historic garrison imaginatively renovated into an elegant 24-room hotel, 2 minutes walk from Carlisle Beach and less than a mile from central Bridgetown.

WEST COAST
Luxury
Sandy Lane, St James, tel: 444 2000, fax: 444 2222,

BARBADOS AT A GLANCE

www.sandylane.com
Barbados's most glamorous
address comes complete
with its own golf course,
spa, four restaurants and
five bars. Fantastically expe-
sive, catering to celebs and
wannabes behind fiercely
guarded privacy walls.

The House, Payne's Bay,
St James, tel: 432 5525,
www.thehousebarbados.com
Small, intimate and chic,
The House has coolly sophisticated décor and a wide
range of complimentary
water sports. Daphne's
restaurant serves modern
Italian food.

Treasure Beach, Payne's
Bay, St James, tel: 419 4200,
fax: 432 1094, www.treasure
beachhotel.com Possibly
the most charming hotel on
the island, a small hideaway
with lush tropical gardens on
magnificent Payne's Bay.
The rooms (all suites) are
large, airy and stylishly
simple. The food is wonderful
and staff delightful. Recently
voted 'Caribbean Small Hotel
of the Year' by *Caribbean
World* Magazine.

Sandpiper, Holetown,
St James, tel: 422 2251,
fax: 422 0900, www.sand
piperbarbados.com Another
of the intimate hotels that
are such a treat for those
with the cash, the Sandpiper
is also set in lovely gardens,
its rooms decorated in cool
'colonial' style. Some suites
have kitchens, and the Tree
Top Suites have private
pools.

Coral Reef Club, Porters,
St James, tel: 422 2372, fax:
422 1776, www.coralreef
barbados.com A wedding-
cake house with gingerbread
balconies, as well as
additional luxury cottages
with their own plunge pools
set in 4.8ha (12 acres) of
beautifully landscaped
gardens. Children welcome.
The fabulous spa is shared by
the Sandpiper, next door.

Cobblers Cove, Speightstown,
St Peter, tel: 422 2291, fax:
422 1460, www.cobblers
cove.com One of the most
northerly hotels, Cobblers
Cove advertises itself as an
English country house on
a Barbados beach, a pretty
mix of flowery design and
Caribbean warmth. Range of
children's activities.

Lone Star, Mount Standfast,
St James, tel: 419 0599,
fax: 419 0597, www.the
lonestar.com Unbelievably,
the Lone Star began life as a
garage. Today, this tiny
boutique hotel, with only
four rooms and a beach
house, is one of the most
sought-after addresses on
the island, frequented by
celebs from Mariah Carey
to John Cleese. If you don't
stay there, at least visit the
restaurant, which is famed
for its spectacular oceanfront
setting and imaginative international menu.

Colony Club, Porters, St
James, tel: 422 2335,
www.colonyclubhotel.com
Colony Club's 96 rooms
and suites are gracefully

furnished; whitewashed
wooden ceilings, bureaus
and rattan rocking chairs.
Some also have four-poster
beds.

**Almond Beach Club Resort
& Spa**, St James, tel: 432
7840, www.almondresorts.
com Large, sophisticated all-
inclusive resort for adults
(16 and over) with several
restaurants and plenty of
entertainment, including a
luxury spa, live music and
convivial company.

Mid-range

Crystal Cove, Appleby,
St James, tel: 432 2683,
fax: 432 8290, www.crystal
covehotelbarbados.com
Attractive family resort
(88 rooms), with plenty of
facilities to keep adults and
children alike entertained,
including a kids' club, live
music and water sports. A
water taxi runs to Tamarind
Cove and the Colony Club.
Top end of the mid-range.

Tamarind Cove, Payne's Bay,
St James, tel: 432 1332,
www.tamarindcovehotel.
com Between The House
and Treasure Beach on lovely
Payne's Bay, Tamarind Cove
is a pleasant family resort
(110 rooms) with several
pools, lovely beachfront and
a range of complimentary
watersports. A water taxi
shuttles guests to other
hotels in the Elegant Group if
they want to try somewhere
different for dinner. Top end
of the mid-range.

Inexpensive
Villa Marie Guesthouse,
Lashley Road, Fitts Village,
St James, tel/fax: 432 1745,
www.barbados.org/villas/
villamarie A friendly little
guesthouse with seven units
(from studios to apartments
for four) and kitchenettes for
self-catering. Surrounded by
lush gardens, 200m (220yd)
from the beach.

Palm Paradise Guesthouse,
Lot 2b, Chapel Gap #1,
Paynes Bay, St James, tel:
422 5430, http://palm
paradise-barbados.com A
little way off the coast and
up the hill, this rambling old
house with lovely gardens
has been turned into a guesthouse with six rooms and
one apartment by its English
expat owner. There's a small
plunge pool. Rates very low,
with air-con extra (fans are
thrown in). Lunch and dinner
available.

EAST COAST
Luxury
The Crane, Diamond Valley,
St Philip, tel: 423 6220, fax:
423 5343, www.thecrane.
com The only up-market
hotel on the east coast, on
the cliff top about 90 steps
above the beach, with a
spectacular pool popular
for fashion shoots. Built in
the 19th century, it is being
dwarfed by a huge time-share
development that is curr-
ently swamping the hotel's
excellent restaurants.
Booking is essential even if
you are staying as a guest.

Plan ahead for their gospel
Sunday brunch.

Inexpensive
Atlantis Hotel, Tent Bay, St
Joseph, tel: 433 9445, www.
atlantishotelbarbados.com
Colonial chic in a restored
seafront boutique hotel with
8 rooms and 2 cottages,
also renowned for excellent
food and lavish twice weekly
buffets.
There are no TVs, radios or
phones in the following
two hotels (by choice).

Sea-U Guest House,
Bathsheba, St Joseph,
tel: 433 9450, fax: 433 9210,
www.seaubarbados.com
A delightful, wood-built
colonial-style hideaway, run
by a German travel writer as
an extended house party.
There are only six rooms or
cottages, with fans, muslin
and mahogany, all with
kitchenettes. Unfortunately
there's no pool, but the sea is
at the bottom of the cliff, and
is within walking distance.

The Round House,
Bathsheba, St Joseph,
tel: 433 9678, fax: 433 9079,
www.roundhousebarbados.
com There are only four
simply furnished rooms at
this small, family-run hotel
with a popular restaurant
serving Bajan specialities.
Live music, from reggae
to jazz, on some evenings.
Reservations are required
on Sundays, but strongly
recommended at other
times too.

SOUTH COAST
Luxury
Little Arches Hotel, Enterprise
Coast Road, Christ Church,
tel: 420 4689, fax: 418 0207,
www.littlearches.com Chic
and friendly family-run
boutique hotel, with just 10
rooms. With hot tubs, a mini-
spa, a romantic rooftop
restaurant and inspired
design (wrought-iron four-
posters, pottery basins) it is
a romantic treat. No children
under 16.

Mid-range
Bougainvillea Beach Resort,
Maxwell Coast Road, Christ
Church, tel: 418 0990, fax:
428 2524, www.bougainvillea
resort.com This 138-room
all-suite resort on Maxwell
Beach is a five-minute walk
from Oistins. Slightly tired,
but the facilities are good and
it remains popular with tour
groups and wedding parties.
Self-catering possible.

Accra Beach Hotel, Accra
Beach, Christ Church, tel: 435
8920, fax: 435 6794, www.
accrabeachhotel.com This
popular three-star south coast
resort hotel has expanded to
224 rooms. Facilities available
for the handicapped.

Inexpensive
Peach and Quiet, Inch
Marlow, Christ Church, tel: 428
5682, fax: 428 2467, www.
peachandquiet.com Friendly
22-room hotel on the beach
near the airport with bright,
simple but comfortable rooms,
a pool and good food.

BARBADOS AT A GLANCE

Surfers Point Guesthouse, Inch Marlow, Christ Church, tel: 428 7873, www.barbados surfholidays.com Seven self-catering apartments at a surf school, so be prepared for obsessive wave talk. Inexpensive to mid-range.

CENTRAL BARBADOS
Mid-range
Lush Life Nature Resort, Suriname, St Joseph, tel: 433 1300, fax: 435 1314, www. lushlife.bb A totally different experience in the lush green hills at the heart of the island. Fabulous views complement 10 beautifully and individually decorated wooden cabins. Wander around the flower farm, take time for a spa treatment and dine at Naniki's, which also does a wonderful jazz brunch on Sundays.

SELF-CATERING
There are several apartment blocks on the beachfront, most available through package tour operators. If you want to be independent, on-line agencies www.holiday rentals.co.uk and www.villa renters.com offer a range of self-catering villas and apartments, many with real charm and character and some at very reasonable prices. There are also lists of properties on the tourist office website, www.barbados.org

WHERE TO EAT
Most of the hotels offer great food. Restaurants have been mentioned where they add something truly special, so *see also* Where to Stay.

BRIDGETOWN
Mid-range
Lobster Alive, Bay Street, tel: 435 0305, http://lobster alive.net Popular seafood place at the beach offering – among other fishy dishes – lobsters fresh from the tank. Open Tue 18:00–21:00, Wed 12:00–16:00, Thurs 12:00–16:00, Fri and Sat closed, Sun 12:00–16:00, Mon closed.
Waterfront Café, Careenage, tel: 427 0093, www.water frontcafe.com.bb Excellent Bajan food served by the water. Live steel pan and jazz music most evenings. Open Mon–Wed 10:00–17:00, Thurs–Sat 10:00–22:00.
Brown Sugar, Aquatic Gap, Needham's Point, St Michael, tel: 426 7684, www.brown sugarbarbados.com Lush décor, a candlelit terrace, great Bajan food and a lunch buffet make it a popular hangout near the Garrison. Reservations recommended. Open 12:00–14:30, 18:00–21:30 (22:00 in season).

WEST COAST
Luxury
The Cliff, Fitts, St James, tel: 432 1922, www.thecliff barbados.com Exquisite food and location – and the price reflects it. Frequently listed as one of the best restaurants in the Caribbean. Reservations required. Open Mon–Sat, plus Sun in high season.
The Tides, Balmore House, Holetown, St James, tel: 432 8356, fax: 432 8358, www.tidesbarbados.com Sitting at the water's edge, this elegantly simple restaurant is heavy on seafood but also caters for the international palate.
The Fish Pot, Little Good Harbour, Shermans, St Lucy, tel: 439 3000, www. littlegoodharbourbarbados. com/dining.html Part of the delightful mid-range Little Good Harbour Hotel, this friendly seafood restaurant in a restored 18th century fort is a popular local favourite for long lazy beachfront lunches and romantic evenings.
Mullins Restaurant and Bar, Mullins Bay, St Peter, tel: 422 2044, www.royalwestmore-land.com/estate/beach/mull-ins-beach-bar The local beach bar went sharply up-market when it was taken over by the Royal Westmoreland Hotel. It's still a beach bar, but definitely the gourmet kind.

Mid-range
Cariba Restaurant and Bar, No. 1 Clarke's Gap, Derricks, St James, tel: 432 8737. The Asian-Bajan fusion food set in a backstreet chattel house has had the gourmet glitterati gossiping since this little restaurant opened in 2008.
Zaccios, Holetown, St James, tel: 432 0134, www.zaccios. com Beachfront restaurant with relaxed atmosphere. International cooking. Take-

away service. Early dinner from 17:30 for families with young children.

Elbow Room, 2nd Street, Holetown, St James, tel: 432 1927. The restaurant is small, the concept is simple – a choice of salads, meats and seafood which arrive raw with a piping hot lava stone for you to do your own cooking at the table. Friendly, laid-back and entertaining.

Paulo's Churrasco do Brasil, Bagatelle Great House, St Thomas, tel: 421 6767, www. paulos.bb A carnivore's feast, Latin American style, in one of the island's grandest plantation homes, also the location of the elegant Chatters Tearoom. There's a second branch of Paulo's on the south coast at St Lawrence Gap.

The Mews, First and Second St, Holetown, tel: 432 1122, http://www.themewsbarba-dos.com/ Small restaurant with eclectic continental menu; it doubles up as a popular after-dinner drinking spot. Live entertainment on Friday and Saturday nights. Booking advised.

Inexpensive
Fisherman's Pub, Queen Street, Speightstown, St Peter, tel: 422 2703. Unpretentious and popular – choose from the Creole buffet or bar menu while you listen to live Calypso music.
Surfside Restaurant and Beach Bar, Holetown, St James, tel: 432 2105. One

of the oldest running beach bars in the area, strictly for sports fans – five monitors show continuous sport, with an additional two plus a 6m (20ft) screen added for major events. Outside tables for non-sports fans. Open daily 09:00–23:00.

Patisserie Flindt, 1st Street, Holetown, St James, tel: 432 2626, www.flindtbarbados. com Ideal for those with the munchies. Paninis, cap-puccinos, gooey cakes and Häagen-Dazs to eat on the terrace or take out. Open Mon–Fri 08:00–17:00, Sat 07:30–16:30, Sun 07:30–12:00.

EAST COAST
Luxury
Zen at The Crane, St Philip, tel: 423 6220, fax: 423 5343, www.thecrane.com/dining Thai and Japanese cuisine overlooking Crane Beach. Ideal for romantic couples to canoodle over the noodles as there is an option to dine privately. Booking essential. Closed Tue.

Inexpensive
The Cove, Bathsheba, tel: 433 9495. Popular local choice serving filling Bajan lunches that change daily, as well as soups and sand-wiches. Open noon–15:00, Tuesday–Sunday.

SOUTH COAST
Luxury
Josef's, St Lawrence Gap, tel: 420 7638, www.josefsin

barbados.com Elegant coral stone beachfront restaurant, complete with romantic candlelight and oriental fusion cuisine. Also home to Kampai Japanese restaurant.
Tapas, Highway 7, Christ Church, tel: 228 0704, www. tapasbarbados.com Open daily 12:00–late (last orders 22:30). Vibrant beachfront restaurant serving eclectic global menu with tapas and main meals from Caribbean and Thai to Spanish and Italian. Beautifully presented and innovative. Booking advised.

Mid-range
Champers, Torrington, Skeete's Hill, Christ Church, tel: 434 3463, www.cham persbarbados.com Lively waterfront wine bar and res-taurant; extensive wine list.
Café Sol, St Lawrence Gap, tel: 435 9531, www.cafesol barbados.com Loud, cheer-ful and immensely popular bar-restaurant, with excellent Mexican food and margaritas served in copious quantities. Happy hour helps, as does the live music at weekends.
Lucky Horseshoe, Worthing, tel: 435 5825, www.luckyh.com Loud, brash and busy, with a steakhouse and live music in the front and a bar, satellite sports and slot machines at the back. Offering huge steaks and even bigger baked potatoes. Open 24 hours.
39 Steps, The Chattel Plaza, Hastings Main Road, Christ

Church, tel: 427 0715, www.39stepsbarbados.com Open for lunch and dinner, closed Sun. Bistro and wine bar family owned for 20 years, informal yet sophisticated. Caribbean and international food with constantly changing specials menu.

Inexpensive

Bubba's Sports Bar and Restaurant, Rockley Main Road, Christ Church, tel: 435 6217, www.bubbassportsbar.net Chomp on hearty portions of the burger and steak variety served while big screens and TVs show US and European sports.

Oistins, the absolute must for south-coast eating is the Friday and Saturday nights fish fry at Oistins. *See* page 58.

Bean-n-Bagel, a reliable chain serving coffee, bagels and muffins, found in several towns on the island.

Chefette, www.chefette.com the island's homegrown fast-food chain, with surprisingly good burgers, salads, etc., in 13 outlets across the island.

Terasu Kafe, Wine World Complex, Rockley, Christ Church, tel: 622 1790, www.terasubarbados.com Inexpensive traditional Bajan fare, breakfast, lunch and dinner, hearty seafood dishes in a relaxed atmosphere. From sandwiches to curries, full of flavour and flair.

NIGHTLIFE

Many of the hotels and restaurants offer live music in the evenings. Most nightclubs can be found on the south coast, along Bay Street and St Lawrence Gap, and feature live bands most nights of the week. One of the main draws for tourists after dark is **Harbour Lights** (Bay St, Bridgetown, tel: 436 7225, www.harbourlights-barbados.com), a nightclub on the beach that is especially popular on Mondays and Wednesdays for its beach extravaganza dinner shows, with everything from stilt walking and fire-eating to steel bands and free-flowing rum punch. They also offer free drinks post-Oistins on Friday nights! Others include:

The Boatyard, Bay Street, Bridgetown, tel: 436 2622, www.theboatyard.com This is the place to let your hair down. By day a beach club, by night live bands. DJs and dancing; Tue, Wed and Fri party nights.

Old Jamm Inn, St Lawrence Gap, tel: 428 3919, http://www.theoldjamminn.com Great burgers, 2-4-1 rum, a laid-back atmosphere and fabulous live music from reggae to soca and jazz alongside the DJs.

Reggae Lounge, St Lawrence Gap, tel: 435 6462. Bop under the stars and the palm trees to a mix of contemporary and old Jamaican tunes, with live music on Thursdays and Sundays. Open 20:00–24:00.

Sugar Ultra Lounge, St Lawrence Gap, tel: 420 7662, www.facebook.com/Sugarbarbados Open Thurs and Sat 22:00–04:00. Slick indoor/outdoor dance club at its best, mixing mainly Caribbean sounds – soca, reggae, hiphop etc. Occasionally attracts homegrown and visiting celebs, so keep watching. Dress code club chic.

Frank Collymore Hall, Central Bank of Barbados, Spry Street, Bridgetown, tel: 436 9083/4, www.fch.org.bb The premier performing arts venue featuring local and international artists and lecturers.

Holders Festival, various venues, tel: 432 6385, www.holders.net Annual performing arts festival with a season of classical music, comedy, jazz and plays performed by many of the world's greats.

SHOPPING

Barbados offers plenty of opportunities to shop till you drop – from outrageously priced high-end goods (aimed mostly at the well-to-do and visiting celebs) to goods for budget-conscious tourists.

Colombian Emeralds International, 24 Broad Street, Bridgetown, tel: 227 1307, fax: 436 7897, www.colombianemeralds.com (there are also branches at the airport, cruise terminal, and several major hotels and other points on Broad Street). Fine emeralds and other exquisite jewellery including custom designs.

Cave Shepherd, Broad Street, Bridgetown, tel: 431 2121, http://mycaveshepherd. com/ (there are branches in Worthing and Sunset Crest Mall). Cosmetics, clothing, electronics, liquor, crystal and china tax-free.

Tours and Excursions
Naturally, there is plenty to see and do on the island. *See also* What to Do in Barbados, page 91.

Useful Contacts
Island Safari, CWTS Complex, Salters Road, St George, Lower Estate, St George, tel: 429 5337, www.islandsafari.bb 4x4, powerboat and eco walk tours of the island by land and sea.
Jammin' Catamaran Cruises, BTI Carpark, Cavans Lane, Bridgetown, tel: 422 1152, www.jammincats.com Turtle cruises and snorkelling.
Eco Adventures, tel: 234 9010, www.ecoadventures-barbados.com/tours Walking tours, hikes and scenic bus tours led by locals.
Cricket: Kensington Oval, Bridgetown, tel: 436 1397, http://kensingtonoval.org/; Barbados Cricket Association, www.bcacricket.org (*see also* page 92).
Equestrian: Garrison Savannah Race Course, St Michael, tel: 426 3980, www.barbadosturfclub.org
Barbados Polo Club, Holders Hill, St James, tel: 432 1802, http://barbadospoloclub.com

Caribbean International Riding Centre, Cleland Plantation, St Andrew, tel: 422 7433;
Highland Adventure Centre, Cane Field, St Thomas, tel: 431 8928.
Water sports: **Silver Sands Resort** (windsurfing), tel: 428 6001; **Barbados Surfing Association**, tel: 228 5117, www.barbadossurfing association.org
Zed's Surfing Adventures, tel: 428 7873, www.zedssurf travel.com Surf lessons, tours and board hire.
Barbados Surf Trips, tel: 262 1099, www.surf barbados.com Tours, camps, lessons and accommodation for surfers.
Sailing: Rubáiyát Catamaran Cruises, tel: 436 6921, www. rubaiyatcatamarancruises. com
El Tigre, 28 Prior Park Terrace, St James, tel: 417 7245, www.eltigrecruises.com
Silver Moon Charters, 69 Clearview Height, Stage 1, St Michael, tel: 438 2088, http:// silvermoonbarbados.com
Diving: (*see also* page 95)
Barbados Blue, Hilton Hotel, Needham's Point, St Michael, tel: 434 5764, www.divebarbadosblue.com
Reefers and Wreckers, Hwy 1, Speightstown, St Peter, tel: 422 5450, www.scuba diving.bb/
West Side Scuba Centre, Baku Beach, Holetown, St James, tel: 432 2558, www.westsidescuba.com

Golf: Barbados Golf Club, Durants, tel: 428 8463, www.barbadosgolfclub.com
Sandy Lane, Sandy Lane Bay, tel: 444 2000, www.sandylane.com
Rockley Golf Club, Club Rockley Barbados, tel: 435 7873, www.rockleygolfclub.com
Tennis: National Tennis Centre, Wildey, tel: 427 5300.
Rallying: Barbados Rally Carnival, Bushey Park Circuit, St Phillip, www.barbadosrally carnival.com
Concierge services:
ASUWISH Luxury service offering virtually everything, from wedding arrangements to real estate, business, baby sitting and travel arrangements. Suite 3B, Bldg 2, Manor Lodge Complex, Warrens St Michael, tel: 424 1302, fax: 417 0154, www.asu-wish.com
Weddings: Cupid's Way Corpo., 154 Atlantic Shores, Christ Church, tel/fax: 420 4832, www. barbadosweddings.com
Tropical Weddings Barbados, Sunny Isle, Worthing, Christ Church, tel: 430 1077, www. tropicalweddingsbar-bados.com
Estate agents: Bajan Services Ltd, Newton House, Battaleys, St Peter, tel: 422 2618, www.bajanservices.com
Boardwalk Realty Inc., Four Aces, Ocean City, St Philip, tel: 423 4770, www.bribarbados.com

Travel Tips

TOURIST INFORMATION
Barbados Tourist Office,
Harbour Road, Bridgetown,
tel: 427 2623, fax: 426 4080,
www.visitbarbados.org or
www.barbados.org Open
Monday–Friday 08:30–16:30.
Another information centre
can be found at the airport
between the arrivals hall,
before Immigration, and the
departure lounge, and is
staffed daily until the last
flight comes in.

Overseas Offices:
Australia: 10th Floor, 1 Bligh
Street, Sydney, NSW 2000,
tel: +678 2 9221 9988,
fax: +61 2 9221 9800, e-mail:
jcunningham@bigpond.com
Canada: Suite 1010, 105
Adelaide Street West, Toronto,
Ontario M5H 1P9, tel: 416 214
9880, fax: 416 214 9882.
Germany: c/o The Mangum
Group, Sonnenstrasse 9,
D-80331 Munich, Germany,
tel: +49 89 2366 2152,
fax: +49 89 2366 2199,
e.n.kohler@magnum.de
UK: 263 Tottenham Court Road,
London W1T 7LA,
tel: 020 7636 9448,
fax: 020 7637 1496,
btauk@barbados.org
USA: 3440 Wiltshire
Boulevard, Suite 1215,
Los Angeles, CA 90010,
tel: +1 213 380 2198 or 380
2199, toll-free (USA) 1 800
221 9831, fax: +1 213 384
2763, www.barbados.org/usa
btala@barbados.org

EMBASSIES AND CONSULATES
Australian High Commission,
18 Herbert Street, St Clair,
Port of Spain, Trinidad &
Tobago, tel: 628 0695,
fax: 622 0659,
www.trinidadand
tobago.embassy.gov.au
Acting as embassy to all
Caricom nations.
British High Commission,
Lower Collymore Rock,
St Michael, tel: 430 7800,
britishhc@sunbeach.net
http://ukinbarbados.fco.
gov.uk
Canadian High Commission,
Bishop's Court Hill,
St Michael, tel: 429 3550,
www.canadainternational.
gc.ca/barbados-barbade
Embassy of the USA, Wildey
Business Park, Wildey,
St Michael, tel: 247 4000,
http://barbados.usembassy.
gov/
Barbados Embassies Abroad:
Canada: 55 Metcalf Street,
Suite 470, Ottawa, Canada
KIP 6L5, tel: 613 236 9517,
fax: 613 230 4362,
ottawa@foreign.gov.bb
UK: High Commission of
Barbados, 1 Great Russell
Street, London WC1B3JY,
tel: 44 20 7299 7150,
fax: 44 20 7323 6872,
london@foreign.gov.bb
USA: Consulate General of
Barbados, 150 Alhambra Circle,
Suite 1000, Coral Gables,
Florida, 33134,
tel: 305 442 1994,
fax: 305 567 2844,
miami@foreign.gov.bb

ENTRY REQUIREMENTS
All visitors are required
to have a passport valid
for at least six months
after the date of departure.
Citizens of Britain, Ireland,
the USA, Canada, Australia
and New Zealand do not
need a visa and can stay
for up to six months.
Visitors wishing to extend
their stay should apply to:
Chief Immigration Officer,
Immigration Department,
Careenage House, The Wharf,
Bridgetown, Barbados,
tel: 426 1011,
e-mail: imm-dept@
caribsurf.com
Other nationals should
contact their nearest
Barbadian embassy before
departure. It is advisable to
have proof of onward travel
and of adequate funds for
your stay.

CUSTOMS
You can bring 1 litre of hard
alcohol, 200 cigarettes or
100 cigars, or 50 cigars and
cigarettes, the total of which
does not exceed 230 grams,
into the country. All goods
that exceed these limits are
subject to taxes and customs
regulations. All fruits,
vegetables, and plants must
be declared.
British nationals over

the age of 17 years of age may take back:

   1 litre of spirits or 2 litres of fortified wine;
   200 cigarettes or 250g of tobacco;
   up to £390 worth of other goods.

Each returning Canadian resident may take back:

   Alcohol: 1.14 litres of spirits, 1.5 litres of wine or 24 bottles or cans of beer (8.5 litres);
   Tobacco: 200 cigarettes and 50 cigars and 200g of loose tobacco.

For those journeying back to the USA, anyone staying for longer than 48 hours may take back goods up to the value of US$800.

Departure tax: there is a departure tax of B$27.50, but this is usually wrapped up in your travel ticket, so remains invisible unless you arrive on a private yacht.

HEALTH REQUIREMENTS

There are no major vaccinations required, although it is probably advisable to check with your local BTA office for current information.

INSURANCE

A good travel insurance policy, available from most reputable travel agents, should cover all medical costs, including repatriations; the loss, theft, or damage of any belongings and money; cancellation and delay; and third-party damages should you cause an accident while staying on the island.

See also Health Precautions on page 124.

GETTING THERE

By Air: A number of major airlines fly into Bridgetown from the UK and USA including British Airways (www.britishairways.com), Virgin Atlantic (www.virginatlantic.com), American Airlines (www.aa.com), Continental Airlines (www.continental.com), Air Canada (www.aircanada.com), Air France (www.airfrance.com), United (www.united.com) and Caribbean Airlines (www.caribbean-airlines.com). All flights come into Grantley Adams International Airport, Christ Church, which is about 13km (8 miles) east of Bridgetown; airport information, tel: 428 7101; flight information, tel: 428 7101. There are buses from the airport into Bridgetown every 15 minutes, and plenty of taxis. There are regular inter-island hopper flights around the Caribbean by Liat (www.liatairline.com) and Caribbean Airlines.

By Sea: Barbados's international deep-water harbour at Bridgetown (see page 44, and http://cruisebarbados.com/bridgetown port.cfm) is a port of call for a number of British, European and American cruise lines. Several charter yachts are also available for inter-island hops.

WHAT TO PACK

Barbados is in the tropics, so light clothing and sunscreen are definitely advisable. Long-sleeved shirts and long trousers are handy for sun protection, and smart casual attire is preferred at many of the more up-market restaurants. Bathing suits are best for lounging in the beach or by the pool.

MONEY MATTERS

Currency: the currency is the Barbados dollar, divided into 100 cents (coins: 1, 5, 10,25, 50 cents and B$1; notes: B$2, 5, 10, 20, 50 and 100). Both Barbadian and US dollars can be used. If you are using US dollars on the island, your

CONVERSION CHART

From	To	Multiply By
Millimetres	Inches	0.0394
Metres	Yards	1.0936
Metres	Feet	3.281
Kilometres	Miles	0.6214
Square kilometres	Square miles	0.386
Hectares	Acres	2.471
Litres	Pints	1.760
Kilograms	Pounds	2.205
Tonnes	Tons	0.984

To convert Celsius to Fahrenheit: x 9 ÷ 5 + 32

change will usually be given in Barbadian currency.

Currency Exchange: the Barbadian dollar (B$) is tied to the US dollar at a rate of B$1.99 to US$1. The exchange rate with the pound sterling is around B$3 to UK£1 (subject to fluctuations).

Changing Money: most of the local banks have automatic teller machines (ATMs) that will accept foreign cards.

Traveller's Cheques: these can generally be exchanged at the banks.

Credit Cards: all the well-known international credit cards are accepted in most places on the island.

Cost of living: the island of Barbados is one of the premier destinations in the Caribbean and the prices clearly reflect this, particularly when it comes to accommodation. For a night's accommodation, you can

---

PUBLIC HOLIDAYS

1 January: New Year's Day
21 January: Errol Barrow Day
Good Friday
Easter Sunday
Easter Monday
28 April: National Heroes Day
1 May: Labour Day
8th Mon after Easter:
Whit Monday
1 August: Emancipation Day
1st Monday in August:
Kadooment Day
1st Monday in October:
United Nations Day
30 November: Independence Day
25 December: Christmas Day
26 December: Boxing Day

---

expect to spend US$45–55 for a guesthouse and US$2500 or more at the luxurious resorts on the west coast. You can otherwise live quite cheaply if you're prepared to travel by public transport and eat mostly in the beach bars. A budget of US$40 a day should cover most of your requirements on the island. However, if you want to have some fun as well as a nice meal, do some sightseeing and be entertained in the evening, expect to spend upwards of US$80 a day. If you have no budget, there are of course plenty of ways to enjoy yourself here.

Tipping: a service charge is automatically added at many of the island's restaurants. Where a service charge is not included in the total, add a 10–15% tip. Some hotels run a 'pay once as you leave' staff kitty.

Tax: 15% VAT is standard; it is usually included within the price quoted. Hotel rooms will have 7.5% VAT and 10% service charge added to the bill.

Duty-free shopping: many of the island's shops offer duty-free shopping as long as you can produce a passport or travel documents and prove you are not a permanent resident of the island. Some goods, such as alcohol, tobacco, and electronics, will be delivered to your plane on your departure; you can take others, such as jewellery or fashion, with you.

ACCOMMODATION

The island offers a wide range of accommodation, from inexpensive guesthouses to some of the world's finest hotels. The west coast is home to many of the pricier luxury resorts, especially around Paynes Bay, while the south coast is a better bet for value accommodation. Staying around Worthing and the nightlife of St Lawrence Gap are popular with the younger crowds, as are the windsurfing hotels in Silver Sands.

Many hotels offer all-inclusive options, but it is generally better value to pay for a room and make the most of the island's restaurants. If you would rather go it alone, villas (with staff) and apartments are also available as self-catering options. For listings, *see* At a Glance, page 113.

EATING OUT

Barbados cuisine is made up of an array of influences, from African to British to Indian, and is unsurprisingly heavy on seafood. Flying fish, Barbados's national dish, is abundant, with shrimp, dorado and snapper also common in the island's invariably good (and often award-winning) restaurants and beachside pubs alike. Traditional Bajan dishes such as pepperpot (spicy meat and okra stew), pudding and *souse*, and *cou-cou* (cornmeal and okra pudding) are very popular indeed, but vegetarians may struggle to find non-meat options, even in side dishes such as peas and rice.

Many of the restaurants, bistros, cafés and pubs serve international cuisine (French, English, Chinese and Mexican), and will also entertain you with calypso, jazz or steel drums. For listings, *see* page 116.

TRANSPORT

The roads in Barbados are good, if rather busy, and distances are short, so hiring a car is a good – although pricey – way of getting around. Prices generally start at around B$135 per day for a Mini Economy (B$550 a week) and a little more for a slightly bigger car. There are a number of car-rental firms on the island, all of which will provide you with a mandatory local driving permit (B$10), and a free road map of the island.

Car Rental: prices generally start at around US$80 a day ($350 per week) inclusive for a small car such as a Suzuki Celerio, and a little more for a slightly larger car. Some of the better rental firms include Coconut (tel: 437 0297, www.coconutcars.com), Jones (tel: 425 6637, www.jonescarrentals.com), Stoutes (tel: 416 4456, www.stoutescar.com), and Rhino Car Hire (UK tel: 0845 508 9845, US tel: +1 888 882 2019, www.rhinocarhire. com), which offers some of the cheapest deals on the island. All firms are based in Bridgetown or at the airport but will deliver to your hotel or elsewhere on the island.

Mopeds/motorcycles: mopeds and motorcycles are another popular way of seeing the island, but helmets and a valid motorcycle licence are legal requirements, while bicycles are a pleasant but not particularly popular method of transport, perhaps due to the narrow, shoulderless roads.

Driving regulations: drivers must be over the age of 21, and some car-hire firms require a doctor's certificate if drivers are over 65. Driving is on the left. The roads are mostly good, although the island's narrow causeways, roundabouts and occasional blind corners make it a good idea to pay careful attention while driving here. The speed limit is 80kph (50mph) on the highway, and 60kph (37mph) on other country roads. Always wer seat belts. There are no specific drink/drive laws, but your insurance may not be valid if you are inebriated at the time of an accident. The only 24-hour petrol station is in Bridgetown; elsewhere opening times vary and most close on Sunday.

Buses: there are two sorts of buses. The larger blue buses are the state-run buses that fan out across the whole island. Services are reliable but not that frequent. Along the south and west coast roads, there are also more frequent privately run yellow 'rasta' buses. Just stand beside the road and flag them down. Let the driver know where you want to get off.

Prices on both are a fixed B$2 however long the journey. Exact money is required.

There are also shared minibus taxis that leave from the bus station next to Cheapside Market in Bridgetown. For bus enquiries, tel: 436 6820.

Taxis: taxis, which are identifiable by a Z on their number plates, are a good way of getting around the island, especially at night when roads can be poorly lit and busy.

Your hotel or guesthouse or the tourist office may be able to recommend a local firm, but it is advisable to confirm the rate with the driver before your journey as there are no meters. Some average rates are: airport to Bridgetown harbour, B$46; airport to St Lawrence, B$31; airport to Speightstown, B$73; airport to Bathsheba, B$73. Drivers are generally honest and you should have no problems with inflated fares.

You can find ranks or flag a taxi down in Bridgetown, along the west or south coasts. Elsewhere, you will probably have to telephone and expect to wait up to 45 minutes for your taxi.

Trains: there is no railway on the island.

Maps: these are provided free of charge by most of the reputable car rental firms and hotels as well as the tourist office.

TRAVEL TIPS

Business Hours
Office Hours: generally Mon–Fri, 08:00–16:30.
Banks: Mon–Thu, 08:00–15:00; Fri, 08:00–17:00.
Shops: Mon–Fri, 08:00–17:00; Sat 08:30–16:30 (supermarkets usually open longer).

Time Difference
Barbados is 4 hours behind GMT. In summer, it is on the same time as US Eastern Daylight Time; in winter, it is EST +1.

Communications
Telephone: the phone system is efficient and local calls are free. Most of the phone boxes across the island are now operated either by credit card or pre-paid calling card, available from larger shops in Bridgetown, supermarkets and hotels. It is also possible to rent a mobile phone, buy a local sim card or use a global sim such as www.global simcard.co.uk if wishing to make overseas calls. There is one area code for the entire island, so to telephone Barbados from abroad, dial +1 246 and the local number. To dial abroad from Barbados, dial 011 + country code and number. To dial abroad on a credit card, via Cable & Wireless, dial: 1 800 744 7777.
Internet: if you need to send a fax, e-mail, or telex, speak to your hotel, post office or business centre,

but there are a number of Internet cafés dotted about the island. Many of the hotels, however, offer free Internet access to guests.

Electricity
Electricity in Barbados is 115/230V 50Hz; American-style plugs with two flat pins are standard.

Weights and Measures
The island officially uses the metric system, although a throwback to British rule means that distances and quantities are often given in miles and pounds.

Health Precautions
While no vaccinations or special precautions are necessary, it is indeed advisable to bring along insect repellent and long clothing to protect against dengue fever (transmitted by mosquitoes). If you suspect you may have been infected, avoid aspirin and contact a doctor immediately. The long clothing will also help ward off sunburn, as will plenty of high-protection sunscreen and staying out of the sun when it's at its strongest (11:00–16:00). If you are badly burned or feel dizzy or nauseous, get medical help.
Water here is among the purest in the world, but packing some diarrhoea tablets is always wise. Wear beach shoes in the shallow water and avoid touching the reefs as the coral rocks can scratch and

it is possible to be stung by lurking nasties such as sea urchins or various poisonous fish, from the zebra fish to the potentially lethal stonefish. If you are stung, seek immediate medical help.

Health Services
Barbados has a reasonably high standard of health care, which is easily accessible to all. The main public general hospital is the Queen Elizabeth Hospital (located on Martindales Road, St Michael, tel: 436 6450, www.qeh.gov. bb). All the medical doctors (as well as their specializations) are listed in the Yellow Pages of the *Barbados Telephone Directory*.
If you need more specialist treatment than that available locally on the island, all the necessary arrangements will be made to transfer you off-island, so good medical insurance is strongly advised. Without the appropriate insurance you can be stranded.

Personal Safety
The crime rate on the island is low but, as in any other cosmopolitan area, use your common sense. Watch your belongings, place valuables in the hotel safe, and do not walk alone after dark in deserted areas. Drugs,including cannabis, are illegal, with a 20-year maximum sentence for possession. Women may experience a degree of hassle, but it is generally good humoured and other locals will come to your aid if the pressure distresses you.

TRAVEL TIPS

EMERGENCIES
Ambulance, dial 511.
Police, dial 211.
Fire, dial 311.

ETIQUETTE
Barbadians are sticklers for good manners. Always greet passers-by, anyone you are asking something of, and shopkeepers with 'good morning/afternoon/evening'. It goes without saying to thank people for a service, and tipping is expected (*see* page 122).

LANGUAGE
English is widely spoken, but there is also a local patois with some colourful phrases (*see* panel, page 107).

MEDIA
There are two national daily newspapers, *The Advocate* and *The Nation*. Foreign papers are obtainable via Newspaper Direct, tel: +800 6364 6364, www.newspaperdirect.com There are several useful free tourism publications available, including the annual *Barbados in a Nutshell* (now available as a mobile app from www.mydestination.com) and the twice-yearly *Barbados Holiday Guide*.
There is one TV station, but most hotels have satellite with a range of US and international stations, including CNN and BBC World.

FESTIVALS
Jan: Barbados Jazz Festival.
Jan–Feb: Open House/Garden (*see* page 102).

Feb: Holetown Festival (1 week); Gold Cup racing.
Mar: Holders Opera Season (*see* page 63).
Apr: Oistins Fish Festival and International Fishing Tournament; Congaline Carnival, Barbados Reggae Festival.
May: Celtic Festival (2 weeks); Gospel Fest (1 week).

May–Aug: Crop Over Festival (12 weeks).
Aug: Grand Kadooment.
Oct: Blowin' in the Windies Youth Jazz Festival (I week); Barbados Film Festival; Taste of Barbados (10 day gourmet food festival).
Dec: Run Barbados (sports festival culminating in the Barbados marathon).

GOOD READING

HISTORY AND HERITAGE
Multiple authors (1990) *A–Z of Barbadian Heritage*. Heinemann.
Alleyn, Warren, and Sheppard, Jill (1999) *The Barbados Garrison and its Buildings*. Macmillan.
Beckles, Hilary McD (2006) *A History of Barbados: From Amerindian Settlement to Caribbean Single Market*. Cambridge University Press.
Callender, Jean H. (1981) *Barbadian Society: Past and Present*. Cave Hill.
Carrington, Sean (2007) *Wild Plants of Barbados*. Macmillan Caribbean Pocket Natural History.
Ferguson, James (1998) *A Traveller's History of the Caribbean*. Windrush Press.
Ligon, Richard (1970) *A True and Exact History of the Island of Barbados* (written in 1657). Frank Cass & Co.
Marshall, Trevor (1981) *Folk Songs of Barbados*. Cedar Press.
O'Callaghan, Sean (2001) *To Hell or Barbados: The Ethnic Cleansing of Ireland* The story of Cromwell's Irish slaves. Brandon/Mount Eagle Publications Ltd.

LITERATURE
Brathwaite, Edward Kamau – the works of this Barbadian poet include *Islands, Masks, Rights Of Passage* and the auto-biographical *Sun Poem*.
Callender, Timothy (1991) *It So Happen*. Heinemann. Humorously moral short stories about rum shop life.
Clarke, Austin (1980) *Growing Up Stupid Under the Union Jack*. McClelland & Stewart. Growing up in colonial Barbados.
Collymore, Frank (1993) *The Man Who Loved Attending Funerals and Other Stories*. Heinemann.
Drayton, Geoffrey (1972) *Christopher*. Heinemann. A young white planter's son discovers the outside world.
Fermor, Patrick Leigh (1984) *The Traveller's Tree: A Journey through the Caribbean Islands*. Penguin. The Caribbean in 1947 through the eyes of one of the great 20th-century travel writers.
Gillespie, Kay (2003) *Tropical Cock Tales with a Twist: Tales of Old Barbados*. Old stories retold. LMH Books.
Lamming, George – anything by this Barbadian novelist whose works include *In The Castle Of My Skin, Natives Of My Person, Season Of Adventure* and *The Pleasures Of Exile*.

125

INDEX

Note: Numbers in **bold** indicate photographs

INDEX